Protecting Historic Coastal Cities

NUMBER THIRTY-FOUR

Gulf Coast Books

Sponsored by Texas A&M University–Corpus Christi

Larry McKinney, General Editor

John W. Tunnell Jr., Founding Editor

Protecting Historic Coastal Cities

Case Studies in Resilience

Edited by Matthew Pelz

TEXAS A&M UNIVERSITY PRESS
COLLEGE STATION

First edition

This paper meets the requirements of ANSI/NISO Z39.48–1992 (Permanence of Paper).
Binding materials have been chosen for durability.
Manufactured in China through FCI Print Group.

∞

Library of Congress Cataloging-in-Publication Data
Names: Pelz, Matthew, editor.
Title: Protecting historic coastal cities : case studies in resilience / edited by Matthew Pelz.
Other titles: Gulf Coast books ; no. 34.
Description: First edition. | College Station : Texas A&M University Press, [2019] | Series: Gulf Coast Books ; number thirty-four | Includes bibliographical references and index.
Identifiers: LCCN 2019011673| ISBN 9781623497705 (book/flexbound : alk. paper) | ISBN 9781623497712 (e-book)
Subjects: LCSH: Coastal zone management. | Historic preservation. | Historic buildings--Conservation and restoration. | Buildings--Natural disaster effects. | Natural disasters--Gulf Coast (US)
Classification: LCC HT391 .P76 2019 | DDC 333.91/7--dc23 LC record available at https://lccn.loc.gov/2019011673

A list of titles in this series is available at the end of the book.

Contents

Acknowledgments

The Galveston Historical Foundation (GHF) would like to thank the authors who have contributed their time and expertise to make this book possible. Each of them demonstrated his or her dedication to spreading knowledge freely and without reservations.

Protecting Historic Coastal Cities is one result of years of effort by staff and volunteers of the GHF and a group of collaborators who have joined us to explore the relationship between the natural environment and the built environment. We would like to thank members of the GHF Green Revival Committee, including Amber Anthony, Chris Arneson, Brax Easterwood, Catherine Gorman, Michael Guillot, Mardi Mitchell, John Prochaska, Chula Ross Sanchez, Tom Schwenk, Lauren Scott, and Brittany Wallace, who cultivated and refined the organization's sustainability and resiliency programs. The group's work to develop the Living on the Edge conferences brought the GHF into contact with each of the contributors to this book as well as dozens of other experts from numerous disciplines. Michael Guillot and Lauren Scott deserve special recognition for their leadership in developing the first conference program.

Other important partners in developing our resiliency programs include the City of Galveston, Building Solutions, Entergy, the National Trust for Historic Preservation, National Trust Insurance Services, the National Center for Preservation Technology and Training, the National Endowment for the Arts, the Galveston Branch of the US Green Building Council, and AIA Houston.

Several experts in history and science fields have donated their time and energy to share their expertise with us. In addition to this book's authors, we would like to thank Kim Anderson, Jerry Androy, Kayode Atoba, Kristopher Benson, Jim Blackburn, Samuel Brody, Dennis Carlberg, David Crossley, Eric Doehne, Elizabeth English, Jens Figlus, Walter Gallas, Kathleen Garland, James Gibeaut, Jessica Grannis, Kate Herbst, Kristen Holley, J. Scott Howell, Chris Hutson, Sarah Jackson, John Jacob, Anne-Lise Knox Velez, Mary Delaney Krugman, Rick Lewis, Tom Linton,

Paul Mardikian, Doug McLean, Aubrey Miller, William Mobley, Tom Murphy, Bob Paterson, Rhonda Price, Jimmy Price, John Prochaska, Chris O'Shea Roper, Roderick Scott, Patrick Sparks, Anne T. Sullivan, Georgeen Theodore, Sharon Tirpak, Amanda Tullos, and Jeana Wiser.

Protecting Historic Coastal Cities

Figures 1.1 and 1.2. In September 2008, Hurricane Ike flooded historic neighborhoods across Galveston Island. The Strand and the East End, both National Historic Landmark districts, were hit especially hard.

Introduction

Galveston Island and Hurricane Ike

W. Dwayne Jones

In the hours after midnight on September 13, 2008, Hurricane Ike crossed Galveston Island, leaving unprecedented damage to the island's historic resources. Residents of the island are not unfamiliar with hurricanes, but Ike caught many unprepared. Despite efforts by local preservationists to educate people, make plans, and project possible outcomes of future hurricanes before 2008, the storm surge from Ike inundated blocks of the city's historic commercial and residential neighborhoods, leaving hundreds of properties devastated from the water. The emotional toll, coupled with the physical damage, paralyzed property owners. Many wondered what could be done and whether historic Galveston would ever return.

The poststorm despair eventually turned into resiliency for residents of the island. A prevailing question was how we could return our historic properties and areas back to their pre-Ike or better condition. The Federal Emergency Management Agency (FEMA) initiated a long-range planning effort that invited local residents and community leaders to envision a new Galveston. An unprecedented total of several hundred Galvestonians showed up for these early meetings and volunteered for committees. At the end, the "new Galveston" plan placed preserving historic properties near the top of local priorities.

The weeks and months that followed Ike offered a number of lessons for those of us who remained on the island. Preservation took on a new and higher level of priority. The rapid pace of removal of properties and materials was at times staggering. Piles of debris removed from buildings would appear at the curbside and disappear within hours, being transported to a large debris holding field at Broadway and 58th Street. It was heartbreaking to see irreplaceable, nonrenewable building materials—longleaf pine, cypress, wainscoting, and stairways—crushed by mechanical jaws and disappearing into the bed of a trash truck.

The staff and volunteers of the Galveston Historical Foundation (GHF) and city staff could not get ahead of the movement to remove, destroy, and replace our historic properties. Professional remediation companies swarmed the island immediately after Ike, and for months afterward their presence was constant and unnerving. State health code required the removal of any building materials up to a foot above flood lines. The state agencies, however, wrote the code for materials of the late twentieth century, not the nineteenth. No language in the code suggested an exception for historic properties and materials. The remediation companies licensed in Texas rarely slowed their destruction. Common sense was not at play, so materials were not being examined and cleaning and drying were not occurring. Cypress siding that I describe as the "Hardie-Plank siding of the nineteenth century" could easily handle water and would, in time, dry. The same was true of the high-quality pine and oak found on many properties.

Even with buckets of cleaning supplies provided by the United Methodist Church and distributed by the GHF, and brochures or leaflets on

Figure 1.3. The 1861 US Custom House, then headquarters of the Galveston Historical Foundation, received heavy flood damage.

Figure 1.4. Flooded materials were subject to mold in the weeks after the hurricane. Confusion as to proper treatment of historic building materials and furnishings complicated cleanup efforts.

preservation strategies in flood areas (we borrowed many items from New Orleans), our preservation troops could not penetrate quickly enough to catch many property owners. As the weeks and then several months passed, communications improved among all parties, and some owners began to clean and wait to dispose of their building materials. Several public forums hosted by the GHF and city leaders provided additional information and offered techniques to preserve our historic properties.

The most substantial impact from Ike fell on the owners of historic properties who were in marginal income brackets. The neighborhoods at the center of the island contain some of the oldest properties, and many of them showed signs of years of deferred maintenance. Owners on fixed or limited incomes deferred care in many cases, and if properties were passed down through generations, the owners did not carry insurance. I call these the "vulnerable populations with vulnerable historic properties." From most anyone's calculations, property owners, and tenants in some cases, were some of the last to return to their homes. These vulnerable populations, the quiet majority, accepted conditions brought by floodwater and wind, adjusting life and accommodations for months after Ike. The federal government programs to assist this population and their property appeared slowly and fell into years of bureaucratic paperwork and "on again, off again" conditions. The state and federal agencies subcontracted responsibility to companies that follow natural disasters across the country and often hire unqualified personnel to fill "required" professional positions. Sometimes even with the best of intentions, these companies repeatedly created obstacles to participation by this vulnerable population. Property owners willingly and then unknowingly fell into line and waited patiently while adapting to the damage and compromised domestic environments. The degree of adaptability by these vulnerable property owners was incredible and sometimes went beyond reason as more prosperous owners repaired property and claimed insurance proceeds.

As I reflect on the months that followed Hurricane Ike, I recall asking why we preservationists do not discuss, train for, or plan for natural disasters. Various professional and paraprofessional organizations host workshops and sessions on natural disasters, but I understand that attendance is low and the call to action fairly weak. Several key learned experiences from Ike began to form in my mind. First, each disaster is different, though some are similar. Experienced FEMA personnel will tell you that the response period is key to understanding the scope and specifics of a disaster, in our case a hurricane. The "event," as it is officially called by FEMA, becomes a description repeated thousands of times in paperwork and claims. That description provides the unique characteristics that drive approaches to recovery as well as funding from both insurance and government.

Second, the emotional toll on the human population, including aid personnel, is not comparable to any other lived experience. Property owners often lose irreplaceable family possessions as well as a sense of worth, along with suffering devastation to their homes, community entities, and businesses. All the familiar places and people shift or disappear, resulting in trauma and uneasiness. One of the most important things I recognized was that community icons and historic properties play a critical role in our sense of place and community. The return of some community icons or institutions (churches, businesses, historic properties) increased the sense of optimism and hope among residents and edged the

Figure 1.5. Hurricane Ike left the hull of the 1877 tall ship *Elissa* vulnerable to corrosion in the weeks and months after the event.

community one more step toward normalcy. People affected by disasters and displacement simply want to return to how it was before the event in the full compass of their everyday existence.

Finally, I became aware that while we can prepare as property owners and civic and community organizations for future disasters to some degree, we need to understand the underlying conditions that make us vulnerable as human beings of all income brackets and forms of "ownership" and, for our cause at the GHF, as historic properties and neighborhoods. This led me to conjecture how that can be done. It is clear that the intersection between the natural environment (and its wonders of climate and occasional disasters) and the built or cultural environment that we work with as preservationists has to bring these environments closer together. We need to understand what builders and homeowners of the previous few centuries understood when constructing buildings that responded to location and geographic factors. We have to blend our natural environment with our built environment in order to be more resilient in the future. We also have to think beyond barriers to future disasters, as Galveston did after the 1900 Storm with the seawall construction and grade-raising projects. While physical forms of restraint or management are important, an exploration of more natural techniques that can be implemented right away and without extraordinary expense is necessary in light of ongoing changes to coastal environments around the globe.

The efforts of this publication, our conferences, and programming at the Center for Coastal Heritage are intended to bridge these two often disparate fields of study and explore these more natural techniques. As we understand each area better, we can begin to project strategies to make our lives more flexible and our historic properties and areas more sustainable.

Evolution of the Texas Coast

John Anderson

Texas is unique relative to other parts of the Gulf Coast in its 591-kilometer-long coastline (367 miles), which is composed mainly of barrier islands and peninsulas (coastal barriers). The sand that makes up these barriers is being depleted through time, making the coast highly susceptible to storm impacts and accelerated sea-level rise. Indeed, portions of the coast are changing at an unprecedented rate. We can gain a better appreciation for why these changes are occurring by examining the natural evolution of the coast. This is done using geological data, such as seismic data and sediment cores, which yield a record of coastal evolution, and radiocarbon dating, which provides age constraints on the timing and rate of coastal change.

The evolution of our coast began thousands of years ago in response to changes in global sea level that resulted from the expansion and decay of Earth's vast ice sheets. The most recent growth of these ice sheets began about 100,000 years ago. By the time they reached their maximum size and volume 20,000 years ago, sea level had fallen about 120 meters (~400 feet). At that time, the east Texas shoreline was located nearly 200 kilometers (124 miles) offshore from its current location. Following the glacial maximum, the ice sheets began to melt as Earth shifted into a warming phase. Initially sea level rose rapidly, faster than 9 millimeters per year (mm/yr) (fig. 2.1), resulting in landward migration of the upper Texas shoreline on the order of tens of meters per year and as fast as 60 meters per year. By approximately 5,000 years ago, as the rate of ice sheet decay decreased, the rate of rise slowed to less than 2 mm/yr, and the rate of shoreline migration also decreased. It was during this period of slow sea-level rise that the modern coastal barriers of the east Texas coast formed (fig. 2.1). The sand that nourished these barriers came from offshore, mainly from erosion of large deltas that formed during the falling stage of sea level. Rivers did not contribute directly to the evolving coastal

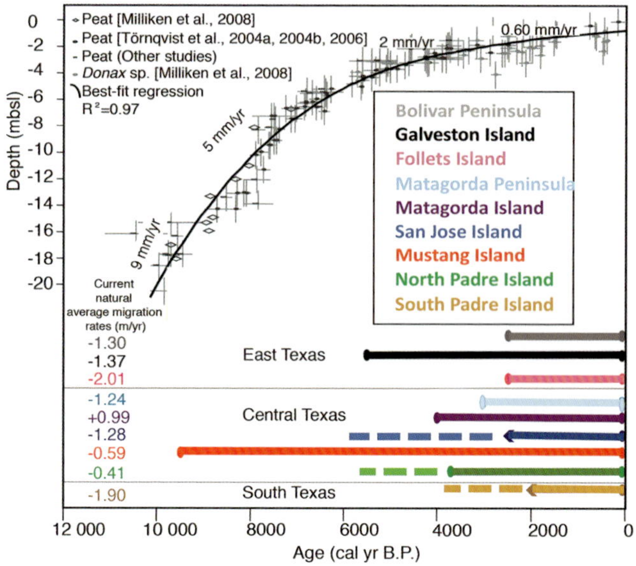

Figure 2.1. Summary of the life spans of coastal barriers, the sea-level curve for the northwestern Gulf of Mexico, and the current natural average shoreline migration rates from the Texas Bureau of Economic Geology. Figure modified and updated from Anderson et al. (2014).

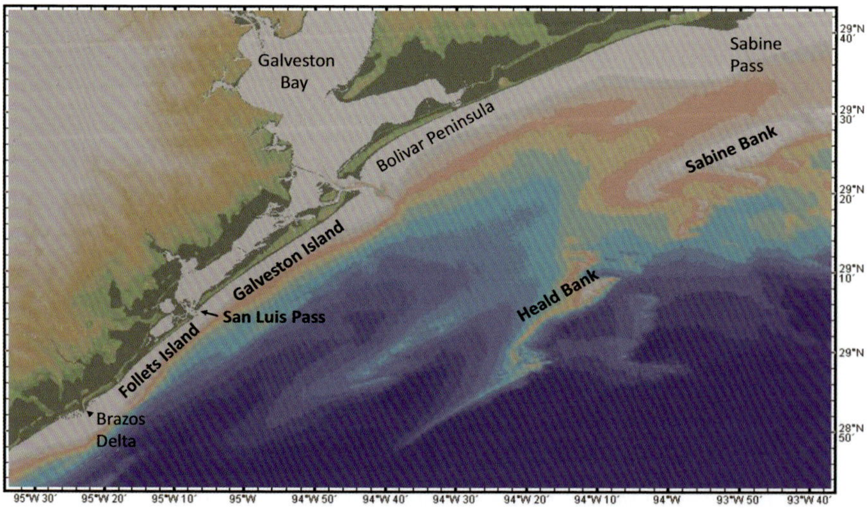

Figure 2.2. Geographic and bathymetric map of the upper Texas coast. Sabine Bank and Heald Bank represent old coastal barriers that were overstepped by rising sea level, leaving them isolated on the continental shelf.

barriers because their valleys were flooded to create the modern bays. As the shoreline migrated landward, the deltaic sources of sand that nourished the coast were overrun by the advancing shoreline, thus shutting off this offshore source of sand. Today, sand supply is restricted and the coastal barriers are shrinking. So, the current landward migration of our coast is partly due to sand starvation, but this does not entirely explain the observed acceleration of shoreline migration in historical time or the variability in shoreline change along the coast.

Like everything else, coastal barriers have a natural aging process—they grow old and eventually die. Remnants of former barrier islands still exist offshore as Sabine Bank and Heald Bank (fig. 2.2), which have retained some of their original barrier characteristics. Radiocarbon ages indicate that Heald Bank was an active barrier 8,000 years ago, while Sabine Bank was active around 6,000 years ago.

The modern coastal barriers of Texas are in very different stages of the aging process. Mustang Island is Texas' most robust and resilient barrier island. It is also the oldest barrier, having reached a ripe old age in excess of 9,000 years (fig. 2.1), and it is over 20 meters thick. During this same time interval, the east Texas coastline has shifted landward some 50 kilometers from its former position at Heald Bank (fig. 2.2). Other coastal barriers have reached old age and are dying. These include Follets Island, Matagorda Peninsula, and South Padre Island. Sediment cores have revealed that the sands that compose these coastal barriers are only one to four meters thick and rest directly on back-barrier bay and lagoon deposits. This indicates that these barriers have retreated significantly from their original locations.

Galveston Island has not reached "old age," but it is no spring chicken when it comes to barrier islands, and it is showing signs that its aging is accelerating. It is the most studied barrier island in the world, thanks to work done decades ago by geologists from Shell Oil Company, who used the island as a model for barrier island evolution that could be used in oil and gas exploration. This work and subsequent studies have shown that the barrier began its life approximately 5,500 years ago as a small island located between the present Strand District and Offatts Bayou. With time, the barrier grew seaward and westward, increasing its width from a few hundred meters to just over four kilometers and extending west to its current location. Sediment cores reveal that growth of the island ceased about 1,200 years ago and the Gulf shoreline began to retreat landward, resulting in the offshore marine mud blanket expanding landward and slowly burying the offshore toes of the barrier. During the first 1,000 years of Galveston's landward retreat, the barrier migrated landward at a rate of about one meter per year. Today, the west end of the island is migrating landward at nearly twice this long-term rate.

Current Changes

As coastal barriers retreat landward they become narrower, lower, and thinner, making them more susceptible to hurricane impact. In particular, storm surge models demonstrate that changes in barrier size, shape, and offshore profile can significantly influence surge. Hence, efforts to predict the impacts of storm surge rely on an understanding of the rate of change to the barriers.

The Texas Bureau of Economic Geology (BEG) is responsible for monitoring changes in shoreline migration over historical time. Its studies have shown that changes along the Texas coast continue to be highly variable. The upper Texas and south Texas shorelines are retreating landward at rates of 0.5 to 4.5 meters per year, the main exceptions being areas where the shoreline has been "stabilized" by human-made structures, areas near tidal inlets, and the Brazos River delta. Historical shoreline change data show that the Mustang Island shoreline has remained relatively stationary through the period of observation, which is about 80 years, while Follets Island, Matagorda Peninsula, and South Padre Island have shoreline retreat rates of two to four meters per year.

The highly variable evolution and historical rates of shoreline change for Texas coastal barriers reflect the different factors that control barrier stability, such as sand supply, sea-level rise, and storm impacts. Stable barriers, such as Mustang Island, are wider, thicker, and higher than their unstable counterparts, which makes them more resilient, allowing them to resist storm breaching and recover more quickly from hurricanes.

As coastal barriers migrate landward, they reach a point in their evolution when much of the sand that is eroded from them is transported across the barrier and deposited in back-barrier bays and lagoons. This process is called *washover*. The rate of washover, measured as the delivery rate of sand from the barrier to the back-barrier setting, is a good indicator of the health of the barrier. The washover rate can also be used to estimate a barrier's life expectancy, the time required for the volume of the barrier to be removed by washover processes, and to estimate the volume of nourishment sand required to stabilize the barrier. Recent research on Follets Island has revealed that its rates of shoreline retreat and washover have increased significantly in historical time. At the current rates of retreat and washover, Follets Island will disappear as a subaerial barrier within three centuries, based on the current rate of sea-level rise and historical storm impacts. The actual life expectancy of the barrier depends on future hurricane frequency and magnitudes, which are not possible to predict. Furthermore, the rate of sea-level rise is expected to double by the year 2100, which will significantly reduce the life span of the island. The fates of Matagorda Peninsula and South Padre Island are equally uncertain, but all indications are that these barriers are nearing the end of their life expectancies.

The Causes of Shoreline Change

We now have good sea-level records for the past 10,000 years (fig. 2.1). These records are derived by radiocarbon dating old marsh and shoreline deposits that are now below sea level. They indicate that the rate of rise for the past 4,000 years averaged 0.6 mm/yr. The actual rate varies regionally because of differences in rates of coastal subsidence. Rates of subsidence along the Texas coast vary from a fraction of 1 mm/yr to over 3 mm/yr. This variability in subsidence is due mainly to variable rates of compaction of soft, water-saturated sediments, which vary from 0 meters to nearly 60 meters thick along the coast.

The current average rate of sea-level rise for the western Gulf of Mexico, derived from tide gauge records and satellite altimetry measurements, is about 2.5 mm/yr. This rate is corrected using available subsidence information. Given the long-term rate of 0.6 mm/yr, the rate of rise has increased about fourfold in historical time. It has been more than 7,500 years since sea level rose at the current rate (fig. 2.1). So, why is the rate of sea-level rise increasing?

The current rate of global sea-level rise is about 3.0 mm/yr. The actual rate varies across the globe because of several variables, but the average rate is based on studies that account for these variables to the degree possible. It is important to note that this 3.0 mm/yr rate matches the rate of rise that is independently estimated from calculations of the expansion of the oceans, based on historical temperature measurements, and estimates of the volume of water produced by glacial melting and ice sheet decay. Yes, the acceleration in sea-level rise is real and its causes are well established. Indeed, it is the most compelling evidence for global climate change.

In summary, there is little question that our coast is changing, and the rate of change has accelerated in historical time. Results from recent research indicate that the main causes of this accelerated change are limited sand supply and accelerated sea-level rise. But other factors must be taken into account when attempting to predict future changes to our coast.

Predicting Coastal Change

To the novice, a change in the rate of sea-level rise of 2.0 mm/yr in historical time does not sound like a lot, and it would take thousands of years for Galveston Island to be drowned at this rate of rise. However, barrier islands do not respond to sea-level rise by drowning in place. Rather, the response is more complicated because of the number of factors that control barrier stability (fig. 2.3). As a result, predicting the fate of a coastal barrier requires complex numerical models along with the data needed to constrain these models.

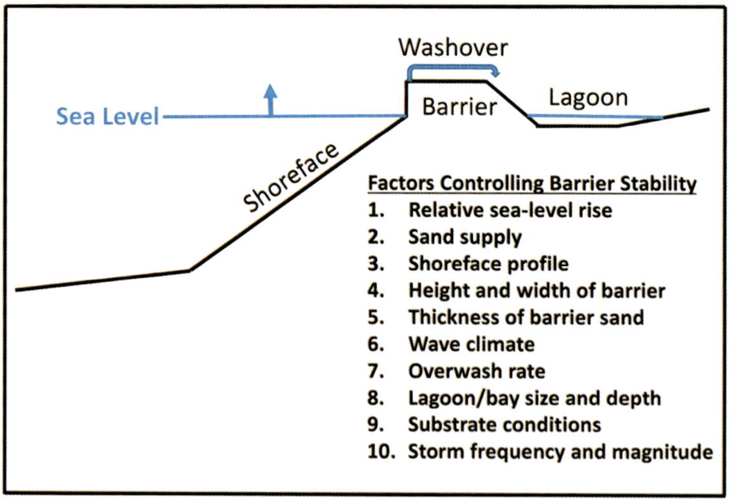

Figure 2.3. Variables that influence coastal barrier stability. These variables must be accounted for when predicting the fate of a coastal barrier.

Other factors being equal, numerical modeling has shown that the response of an island to an increase in the rate of sea-level rise of a few millimeters per year is, in fact, quite significant. For example, an increase in the rate of sea-level rise to 10 mm/yr by the year 2100 would result in a fourfold increase in the magnitude of shoreline retreat. For west Galveston Island, this would result in a rate of shoreline retreat of about six meters per year. A more conservative increase in the rate of rise of 6 mm/yr results in an estimated doubling of the current rate of coastal retreat on Galveston Island.

Of those factors that regulate barrier stability, storm impact is the only one that is not predictable. We know that tropical storms significantly impact coasts, but coastal barriers have a natural ability to heal following storms. This is largely because most of the sand that is eroded from the barrier during storms is not transported far offshore and is ultimately delivered back to the recovering shoreline. Furthermore, there is no historical or geological evidence for an increase in storm frequency and magnitude along the Texas coast, so the observed acceleration in coastal change does not appear to be due to storm impacts.

Research in developing more reliable numerical models for assessing coastal barrier resilience and predicting coastal change is progressing slowly, partly because only a handful of scientists are working on this problem. In Texas, more data are needed to test and improve numerical models. Such data include detailed sand budget analyses that constrain the volumes of sand moving along shore, offshore during storms, into tidal deltas, and into back-barrier bays and lagoons via washover. We also need more measurements of coastal subsidence, the other component of relative sea-level rise, and improved understanding of sand transport processes. Until this work is accomplished, it will not be possible to understand and predict coastal change, to evaluate coastal preservation strategies, and to assess potential solutions for coastal erosion, such as providing the volumes of sand needed to nourish and sustain wetlands and beaches. In summary, it will not be possible to develop a comprehensive coastal management plan for Texas.

Galveston Island Resiliency

While we are still a long way from developing a statewide coastal management plan, significant progress has been made in some areas. Detailed studies have been conducted on the east Texas coast and on Mustang Island, and work is currently underway elsewhere along the central Texas coast. Galveston Island is the most well-studied coastal barrier. The island's sand budget has been constrained, as shown by both numerical analysis (US Army Corps of Engineers) and geological analysis (Rice University). While the results from these two approaches do not agree entirely, they do provide an important step in the right direction, and the lessons learned can be used to develop better sand budgets.

Research shows that relatively little of the sand eroded from Galveston Island is transported to the back side of the island by storm washover. Likewise, sediment cores from offshore of the island contain relatively small amounts of beach-derived sand. Most of the sand that is eroded from the island is transported westward by longshore currents and is ultimately deposited within the San Luis tidal delta (fig. 2.2). Historical charts and radiocarbon ages from sediment cores are used to measure the long-term and historical sand flux to the delta. These results show that the delivery of sand to the tidal delta over the past 2,100 years has been 4,300 cubic meters per year, while the historical rate has been approximately 10,000 cubic meters per year. Thus, the volume of sand that is currently being eroded from the Galveston shoreline is estimated to be more than 10,000 cubic meters per year. This is also a good approximation of the amount of sand needed to stabilize the island. To my knowledge, the only potential sources for this large volume of sand are located tens of kilometers offshore.

Fixing the Problem

Texans tend to have a "we can fix the problem" attitude, even when it comes to global sea-level rise, but we have serious issues with science denial, such as accepting the reality of accelerating sea-level rise and the resulting unprecedented coastal change. Following Hurricane Ike, the concept of the "Ike Dike" was born. The idea here was to construct a massive levee and dike system that would extend from High Island to San Luis Pass to protect inland areas from storm surge. Policy makers immediately grasped the idea, even though there was little hard science or engineering to back the proposal. In fact, eight years after the Ike Dike was proposed, there are still important questions about the size and location of the structure, where the material needed to construct and maintain it would come from, its effectiveness in abating storm surge and poststorm flooding, and its environmental impacts. As we have seen, the amount of sand needed to maintain the Ike Dike if it were constructed at the current shoreline is huge, and no source for that sand has been identified. A more realistic idea would be to raise the elevation of the coastal highways, but this would require a detailed plan for managing traffic flow onto and off the highway and for managing rainwater drainage.

Alternatives to the Ike Dike exist, such as a smaller-scale dike system that would protect the industrial complex in upper Galveston Bay, but these offer little protection for the coast (Rice University SSPEED Center Plan). Other options that warrant study include large-scale beach nourishment using hopper dredges to mine sand from offshore and deliver that sand to the coast. We do know that sufficient volumes of sand exist offshore to nourish our coasts for decades and perhaps even centuries. Here again, little progress has been made during the post-Ike period in assessing these and other coastal protection scenarios, including engineering plans, environmental impact assessments, and economic and social impact analyses. Given the cost of these options, we cannot afford to undertake these assessments while ignoring the changes that are occurring along our coast, nor can we afford to ignore the science.

Additional Reading

This summary is based on results from scientific research that is published in peer-reviewed, international scientific journals and has been recently summarized by Anderson and others (2014). For additional reading on the topic, the reader is also referred Anderson (2007).

Acknowledgments

This chapter is based on results of studies by a number of Rice University graduate students over the past 35 years that are summarized in Anderson et al. (2014). Our current research is funded by the Shell Center for Sustainability at Rice University.

References

Anderson, J. B. *The Formation and Future of the Upper Texas Coast*. College Station: Texas A&M University Press, 2007.

Anderson, J. B., D. J. Wallace, A. R. Simms, A. B. Rodriguez, and K. T. Milliken. "Variable Response of Coastal Environments of the Northwestern Gulf of Mexico to Sea-Level Rise and Climate Change: Implications for Future Change." *Marine Geology* 352 (2014): 348–66.

Texas Bureau of Economic Geology (BEG). https://coastal.beg.utexas.edu/shorelinechange2012/.

Storm Surge

One of the World's Foremost Natural Hazards

Hal Needham

Several major natural hazards threaten coastal regions: earthquakes, volcanoes, and landslides trigger tsunamis, and high-speed waves sometimes build to terrifying heights as they approach coastlines. From a certain perspective, sea-level rise is a slower-paced hazard that threatens to permanently inundate coastlines from thermal expansion of ocean waters and melting of glaciers and ice sheets. On coastlines around the globe, powerful storm surges, occurring as low air pressure and strong onshore winds push water inland, are the most feared weather hazards.

Storm surges are observed anywhere strong onshore winds push water toward land. Tropical cyclones, known as hurricanes in the North Atlantic and Northeast Pacific basins, have generated the highest recorded storm surges. A tropical cyclone striking Bangladesh in 1876 produced the world's highest recorded surge as water levels reached a remarkable level of 44.9 feet.[1] In August 2005, Hurricane Katrina generated the highest recorded surge in the Western Hemisphere as the large, powerful hurricane produced a storm tide of 27.8 feet in Pass Christian, Mississippi.[2]

When large storm surges strike densely populated coastlines, the loss of life is often catastrophic. Therefore, we should not be surprised that storm surges are among the deadliest natural hazards, with annual fatalities ranging from 10,000 to 15,000. The number of fatalities in the most catastrophic events far surpasses the annual average. The 1970 Bhola Cyclone, for example, killed approximately 300,000 people in Bangladesh.[3] The cyclone passed along the Bay of Bengal in the northern Indian Ocean, where the world's deadliest surges have each occurred. In this relatively small basin, six severe storm surge events have inflicted at least 140,000 fatalities.[4]

In the United States, storm surge is responsible for approximately 90 percent of hurricane fatalities.[5] The 1900 Galveston Hurricane generated

Figure 3.1. The 1900 Galveston Hurricane destroyed much of Galveston Island. (Preservation Resource Center, Galveston Historical Foundation, Galveston, Texas).

a 15.7-foot storm tide that destroyed much of Galveston, Texas (fig. 3.1), and contributed to more than 6,000 total fatalities in the city and 6,000 more on the mainland.[6] This event is still the deadliest natural disaster in US history.

In addition to high death tolls, storm surge events are also among the costliest natural disasters. Hurricane Katrina's surge, as a prime example, inundated 80 percent of the New Orleans metropolitan area and caused $157 billion (adjusted to 2018 value) in damage, making Katrina the costliest natural disaster in US history. Hurricane Sandy generated a destructive surge in New York and New Jersey just seven years after Katrina, with damage totaling $73.4 billion in losses.

Physical Processes That Influence Storm Surge

Hurricane-generated storm surges are complex phenomena that are influenced by many circumstances. The complexity of this hazard creates challenges for both forecasting and public education. Variables related to both the storm and the coastal environment influence the nature of storm surges. Storm variables include the minimum central air pressure, maximum sustained winds, and the geographic extent of the wind field. Coastal variables include coastal shape, the bathymetric profile of offshore waters (underwater topography), and the presence of both natural and human-made barriers to flowing water.

Storm Processes That Influence Storm Surge

The minimum central air pressure of a hurricane is inversely related to the storm surge level for two reasons. One is that air pressure is a measure of the atmospheric force pushing down on an object from above; lower air pressure means less force is pushing down on the water, enabling the water to rise. This relationship is sometimes called the *law of the inverted barometer*, or the *inverse barometer effect*. Another reason for this inverse relationship is that wind speeds generally strengthen as a hurricane's air pressure drops, and these intensified winds displace more water to the coastline, raising water levels.

Strong wind is important for generating storm surge, and some sources indicate that it is the most important factor. An exponential relationship exists between maximum sustained winds and storm surge levels, meaning even modest wind intensification will increase water levels on the coast, if all other variables are held constant. This relationship is maximized when correlating storm surge height to prelandfall wind speed, as the wind speed before the hurricane makes landfall is a better indicator of storm surge potential than the wind speed as the hurricane strikes the coast. Storm surge levels correlate best with maximum sustained wind speeds 18 hours before a hurricane makes landfall.

Several geographically large hurricanes during this century have demonstrated the importance of hurricane size for storm surge generation. The most well-known storms are hurricanes Katrina (2005), Ike (2008), Isaac (2012), and Sandy (2012). Hurricane Katrina generated a higher storm surge than Hurricane Camille did in 1969, even though both storms made landfall in coastal Mississippi and Camille produced higher wind speeds. Katrina's large geographic size likely explains the difference in surge heights.

Hurricane Ike generated an extensive storm surge from South Texas to Florida, with water levels reaching as high as 17.5 feet in Chambers County, Texas.[7] This water level surprised many people, considering that Ike made landfall as a category 2 hurricane. Ike's enormous size explains

Figure 3.2. A satellite image of Hurricane Ike approaching the Texas coast. (National Aeronautics and Space Administration, Earth Observatory, 2008)

this massive storm surge event; tropical storm–force winds extended 160 nautical miles and hurricane-force winds extended 110 nautical miles from the center of Ike's circulation (fig. 3.2) as the storm approached the Texas coast.

In 2012, both hurricanes Isaac and Sandy produced severe storm surges that surprised many people, as both storms approached coastlines as category 1 hurricanes. Isaac's tropical storm–force winds extended 207 miles from the center of circulation, enabling the storm to generate a storm tide of 14.1 feet in Louisiana.[8] Two months later, Sandy's staggering tropical storm–force wind field, which extended 483 miles from the center of circulation and covered a straight-line distance of 943 miles,[9] produced a catastrophic storm surge that contributed to 147 storm deaths and $50 billion in damage.

Tropical storm–force winds sustain speeds of 39 miles per hour and are strong enough to down trees and cause widespread power outages. Sandy's extraordinary wind field extended mostly over water, making it difficult to place in context. By comparison, had this wind field developed over land, the diameter of tropical storm–force winds would have extended from Toronto, Ontario, to Jacksonville, Florida.

Coastal Processes That Influence Storm Surge

An inverse relationship exists between storm surge levels and coastal bathymetry. Higher storm surges develop in areas where offshore water is shallower, because underwater currents do not have enough room to redistribute displaced water. This principle is counterintuitive for many people, as it may seem logical that deeper offshore water would produce larger floods.

This dynamic is better understood when considered from the perspective of water displacement in large and small containers. Imagine if we filled a 50-gallon aquarium to the brim with water and then dropped a heavy rock into it. The water displaced by the rock would splash us because it would have nowhere to go but up; it could not move right, left, forward, backward, or down.

Now imagine doing the same experiment in an Olympic-sized swimming pool. We fill the pool to the top and sit as close to the edge as possible without getting wet. Then a mechanical arm drops the same rock into the middle of the pool. We would expect a small wave to ripple out in concentric circles, but we would not expect to get very wet. In this larger container, water has more room to move in various directions, and only a little water splashes out of the container at any given location. If bathymetry in this case relates to the depth of our container, then coastal shape would relate to the walls. When displaced water meets a hard boundary, the water flow is redirected. Think back to the aquarium, which is a small space closed on five sides. The water splashes out of the top quite efficiently because the top is the only open side.

In this way, coastal shape and geometry influence storm surge patterns as well, as water piles up on the windward side of natural or human-made obstructions that protrude from the coastline. Such obstructions can be large or small. For example, the Mississippi River Delta in South Louisiana protrudes sharply more than 60 miles to the south along the northern Gulf Coast. This delta efficiently traps water flowing from east to west along the northern side of hurricanes. Obstructions that influence storm surge are not always this large; seawalls and levees enhance surge on the windward side as well, although their impact is smaller than that of a large delta.

Another counterintuitive aspect of coastal shape is that bays, harbors, and inlets enhance storm surge height as well. This is ironic because such locations provide safe havens for marine interests in normal conditions. However, during a storm surge event, these areas provide efficient "aquariums" that are shallow and bounded on most sides, trapping water and forcing it to rise.

The efficiency with which these coastal factors enhance storm surge levels is quite surprising, because they seem to be "invisible" and are difficult for us to sense. We easily perceive a sudden increase in wind speed and immediately see its effects right in front of us. However, it is difficult for us to perceive water depth. When we stand on a beach and look out at a watery horizon, a seascape that is deep may look the same as a shallow one.

Nonetheless, these factors greatly influence storm surge. Researchers have estimated that Hurricane Katrina's storm surge level would have dropped 13 feet had the storm tracked slightly east and made landfall in neighboring Alabama instead of Mississippi. Such discoveries are of the utmost importance. In this case, it suggests that Katrina's catastrophic surge would not have happened in Alabama, at least not to the extent observed in Mississippi and Louisiana.

These factors explain the localized nature of storm surges. Surge levels in a bay or on the windward side of a levee are sometimes substantially higher than in other coastal locations just several miles away. Storm surge heights along the Mississippi River Delta in South Louisiana during Hurricane Katrina provide an excellent example of localized surge patterns. Water levels to the east of the Mississippi River levees were estimated to be nine feet higher than water levels to the west of the levees, even though the two locations were separated by only several miles.

As humans, we tend to think catastrophic surges have everything to do with the storm that produced them. In reality, the coastal environment, which remains more constant than the atmosphere, plays a major role in storm surge generation. Although coastal zones are dynamic and change rapidly at the microscale, bathymetry, coastal shape, and other factors remain relatively constant.

These principles help explain why the two largest storm surges on record in the Western Hemisphere were both observed near Pass Christian, Mississippi. This location brings together several coastal factors, including shallow bathymetry, the presence of Bay St. Louis, and proximity to the Mississippi River Delta, in an area that is vulnerable to powerful hurricanes.

The Characteristics of Storm Surge

When we think of floods, the most common images that come to mind depict high water inundating the built or natural environment. Yet floods are dynamic events that tell a story beyond our single-frame images. Water can rise incredibly quickly or slowly, filling a city up like a bathtub or flowing through a town like a raging river. Storm surge flooding may begin before the arrival of strong winds, or it may not occur until after the eye of the hurricane passes.

Storm surge timing varies considerably by both location and storm. The shape of the coastline relative to the storm track plays an important role in this timing. In the Northern Hemisphere, broad coastlines that are open to the northeast, east, or southeast often experience storm surge flooding well in advance of hurricanes, as the hurricane wind field has plenty of time to pile up storm surge.

Although prolonged onshore winds commonly pile up water onto windward-facing shores, in some circumstances a prolonged shore-parallel wind will generate an early storm surge, particularly if the coastline is broad and shallow. This process is known as a *forerunner surge*, and it is common on the Texas coast. It was observed during the 1900 and 1915 Galveston Hurricanes as well as Hurricane Ike in 2008. Figure 3.3 depicts water levels at the Pleasure Pier tide gauge on Galveston Island as Ike approached. Although the gauge malfunctioned during the height of the storm, the forerunner surge is visible on the graph.

Although the forerunner surge does not generate the highest water levels in a storm, it is deadly because its arrival cuts off evacuation routes early, trapping people along the coast. These surges can precede the peak surge level by more than 24 hours. Hurricane Ike's forerunner arrived 12–24 hours before the hurricane made landfall, and it reached as high as 10 feet in some areas.

By contrast, storm surges can also occur later in the storm, even after the eye of the storm has passed. In these cases, the surge may form suddenly. The Philippines often observes rapid surge onset because of its configuration as an archipelago of over 7,000 islands. These islands contain many bays and inlets open to the sea in one direction. When a storm track

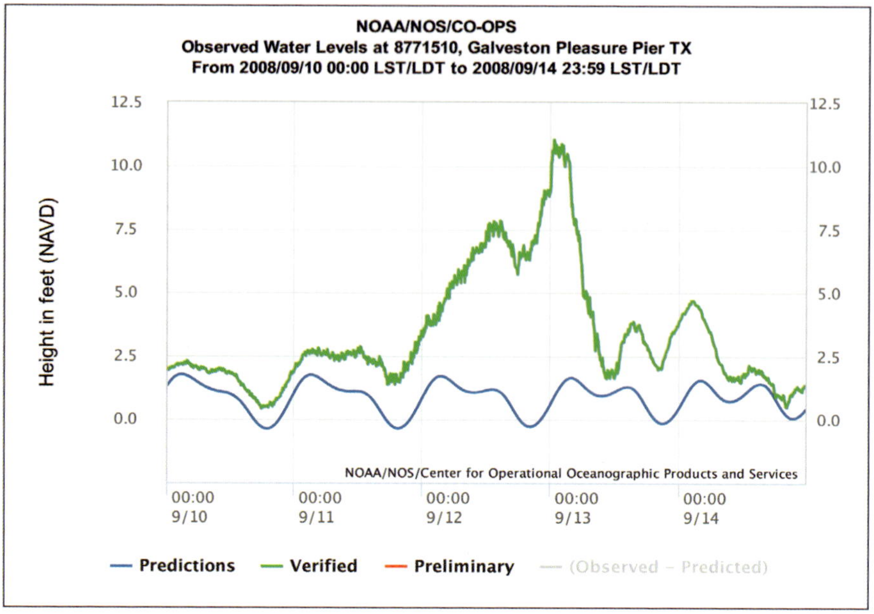

Figure 3.3. This graph of water levels at Galveston's Pleasure Pier tide gauge depicts the occurrence of both forerunner and peak surges during Hurricane Ike. The green line depicts observed water levels, whereas the blue line depicts predicted astronomical tide. (National Oceanic and Atmospheric Administration, 2016)

produces strong onshore winds over one of these bays, surges will rapidly form. Such events were observed in 1908 when a severe cyclone destroyed the town of Tarol,[10] and more recently in the city of Tacloban in 2013.[11] In the latter case, Super Typhoon Haiyan generated a sudden surge near Tacloban after the eye passed, and this raging torrent of water was responsible for many of the 6,300 deaths.

Storm surge levels can also rise rapidly with a sudden change in wind direction. This can happen in Galveston despite the island's broad, gently sloping shoreline, which would otherwise lead to gradual increases in surge height. Dr. Isaac Cline, the official in charge at the Galveston Weather Bureau during the 1900 Hurricane, observed, "The water at this time was about eight inches deep in my residence, and the sudden rise of four feet brought it above my waist before I could change my position."[12]

Waves riding on top of storm surges greatly increase the destructive potential of coastal flooding. Waves break when they "feel" the ocean bottom. Areas with deeper bathymetry experience higher waves than shallow coastlines because in shallow areas the energy (wave) is broken many times before it reaches shore. This explains the pattern of larger waves breaking closer to shore in California compared to smaller waves breaking many times in Mississippi or Texas.

While hurricanes generate high waves, the details of these waves vary by storm and location. Storm waves are often described as chaotic because waves approach from different angles. Also, the same storm may generate different types of waves at different sites. Consider Hurricane Ivan (2004), which generated extraordinarily high waves off the coast of the Florida Panhandle. The waves reached heights of 89 feet, based on the elevation of damage to oil and gas platforms.[13] After considering such mammoth waves offshore, we may be surprised to see a video of small waves flowing rapidly inland as Ivan made landfall during the night.

The fast-flowing water observed during Ivan's landfall was more characteristic of a river than the ocean. In some cases, we may see such water flowing inland even though we are accustomed to seeing it flow toward the sea in normal river settings. While misunderstood, rapidly flowing storm surge water has been well documented in historical literature. Speaking again of the 1900 Galveston Hurricane, Dr. Cline provided a valuable observation related to the phenomenon of fast-flowing surge waters across the landscape. He stated, "I was standing at my front door, which was partly open, watching the water, which was flowing with great rapidity from east to west."

Finally, although storm surge impacts may be most extreme at the coast and in bays, surges sometimes extend inland for great distances in low-lying areas. Such extensive floods are particularly severe because saltwater inflicts long-term impacts, such as losses in production of sugarcane, which is salt intolerant, or deterioration of buildings not constructed with galvanized nails. A tropical cyclone in Myanmar flooded the Irrawaddy River system inland for at least 60 miles in 1975.[14] Storm surge along the US Gulf Coast washed inland more than 37 miles during Hurricane Rita in 2005 and at least 34 miles during Hurricane Ike in 2008.

While topics such as flood timing and duration, the presence of waves, and the extent of inland inundation provide detailed and seemingly nuanced observations, they are important for several reasons. These details provide us with a more colorful account of what coastal flooding is like, and they show us that such events are often not peaceful or gradual. They can also mean the difference between life and death, as the timing of flooding is important for evacuation efforts. It is not possible to generalize storm surges, as one surge event may differ considerably from another, even if the maximum water levels of the two events are similar.

Global and Regional Storm Surge Patterns

A comparison of global storm surge observations is useful in providing context for the severity of these events in different parts of the world. The most severe storm surges, in terms of both physical magnitude and human impact, have occurred along the shores of the Bay of Bengal in the northern Indian Ocean. In this region, 10 recorded storm surges have reached at least 29 feet; the highest reached 45 feet in Bangladesh in 1876.[15] This basin observes an average of five surge events at least 16.4 feet high per decade.

Human losses in the basin have been staggering. Storm surge events in this region have killed at least 140,000 people at least six times in recorded history,[16] including the catastrophic loss of 300,000 people in Bangladesh in 1970. Remarkably, this basin observes only 5–6 percent of the world's tropical cyclones, but 80–90 percent of tropical cyclone fatalities.[17]

The shallow bathymetry and concave shape of the Bay of Bengal create an ideal basin for generating such massive surges. The high population density along this coastline exacerbates the flood impacts, as masses of poor people cannot afford the transportation costs associated with evacuation, or the technological infrastructure, such as computers and the internet, to quickly convey emergency information.

Research has found that along the Gulf Coast, South Florida is the area most vulnerable to severe hurricane strikes (defined as category 3–5 hurricanes), while places such as coastal Mississippi, Louisiana, and Texas are not as vulnerable. For example, Fort Myers and Key West, Florida, experience a major hurricane strike every 15 years on average, which is the shortest return period in the region. However, from Texas to Mississippi the shortest return period is 26 years, observed at Galveston, Texas, as well as at Morgan City and Boothville, Louisiana. Nonetheless, larger storm surges have been observed in Texas, Louisiana, and Mississippi than in South Florida.

In understanding coastal hazards, it is important that we separate the three major hazards of a hurricane—wind, rain, and storm surge—into different analyses. Along the Gulf Coast, we find South Florida most vulnerable to hurricane wind, but the coastlines of Mississippi, Louisiana, and Texas are most vulnerable to hurricane surge. Such generalizations do not ensure lack of catastrophic winds in Texas or surge in South Florida, but they help us understand risk and prepare accordingly.

Notes

1. S. K. Dube, A. D. Rao, P. C. Sinha, T. S. Murty, and N. Bahulayan, "Storm Surge in the Bay of Bengal and Arabian Sea: The Problem and Its Prediction," *Mausam* 48 (1997): 283–304.

2. R. D. Knabb, J. R. Rhome, and D. P. Brown, *Tropical Cyclone Report, Hurricane Katrina, 23–30 August 2005* (National Hurricane Center, December 20, 2005), https://www.nhc.noaa.gov/data/tcr/AL122005_Katrina.pdf.

3. N. L. Frank and S. A. Husain, "Deadliest Tropical Cyclone in History," *Bulletin of the American Meteorological Society* 52 (1971): 438; Dube et al., "Storm Surge in the Bay of Bengal."

4. H. F. Needham, B. D. Keim, and D. Sathiaraj, "A Review of Tropical Cyclone-Generated Storm Surges: Global Data Sources, Observations and Impacts," *Reviews of Geophysics* 53 (2015): 545–91.

5. Policy statement of the American Meteorological Society on hurricanes, as adopted on October 20, 1972, *Bulletin of the American Meteorological Society* 54 (1973): 45–47.

6. David G. McComb, *Galveston: A History* (Austin: University of Texas Press, 1986), 122, 126.

7. R. Berg, *Tropical Cyclone Report, Hurricane Ike (AL092008), 1–14 September 2008* (National Hurricane Center, updated 2014), https://www.nhc.noaa.gov/data/tcr/AL092008_Ike.pdf.

8. B. E. McCallum, B. D. McGee, D. R. Kimbrow, M. S. Runner, J. A. Painter, E. R. Frantz, and A. J. Gotvald, *Monitoring Storm Tide Flooding from Hurricane Isaac along the Gulf Coast of the United States, August 2012*, Open-File Report 2012–1263, http://pubs.usgs.gov/of/2012/1263/.

9. J. Demuth, M. Demaria, and J. A. Knaff, "Improvement of Advanced Microwave Sounder Unit Tropical Cyclone Intensity and Size Estimation Algorithms," *Journal of Applied Meteorology* 45 (2006): 1573–81.

10. C. P. Arafiles and C. P. Alcances Jr., *Storm Surge Potentials of Selected Philippine Coastal Basins*, 1978, http://www.pagasa.dost.gov/ph/research.shtml (site discontinued).

11. *Killer Typhoon*, documentary film originally shown on *NOVA* on PBS, 2014, http://www.pbs.org/wgbh/nova/earth/killer-typhoon.html.

12. I. Cline, "Special Report on the Galveston Hurricane of September 8, 1900," *Monthly Weather Review* 28, no. 9 (1900): 373.

13. G. W. Stone, N. D. Walker, S. A. Hsu, A. Babin, B. Liu, B. D. Keim, W. Teague, D. Mitchell, and R. Leben, "Hurricane Ivan's Impact along the Northern Gulf of Mexico," *EOS, Transactions, American Geophysical Union* 86 (2005): 497.

14. S. K. Dube, A. D. Rao, P. C. Sinha, and P. Chittibabu, "Storm Surges: Worst Coastal Marine Hazard," in *Modelling and Monitoring of Coastal Marine Processes*, edited by C. R. Murthy, P. C. Sinha, and Y. R. Rao (New Delhi: Springer and Capital Publishing, 2008), 125–40, 246.

15. Dube et al., "Storm Surge in the Bay of Bengal."

16. Needham et al., "Review of Tropical Cyclone-Generated Storm Surges."

17. K. M. M. H. Chowdhury, "Cyclone Preparedness and Management in Bangladesh," in *Improvement of Early Warning System and Responses in Bangladesh Towards Total Disaster Risk Management Approach*, edited by BPATC (Savar, Dhaka, Bangladesh, 2002), 115–19; B. K. Paul, "Why Relatively Fewer People Died? The Case of Bangladesh's Cyclone Sidr," *Natural Hazards* 50 (2009): 289–304.

Additional References

Ali, A. "Vulnerability of Bangladesh to Climate Change and Sea Level Rise through Tropical Cyclones and Storm Surges." *Water, Air, and Soil Pollution* 92 (1996): 171–79.

Baade, R. A., R. Baumann, and V. Matheson. "Estimating the Economic Impact of Natural and Social Disasters, with an Application to Hurricane Katrina." *Urban Studies* 44, no. 11 (2007): 2061–76.

Blake, E. S., T. B. Kimberlain, R. J. Berg, J. P. Cangialosi, and J. L. Beven II. *Tropical Cyclone Report, Hurricane Sandy (AL182012), 22–29 October 2012.* National Hurricane Center, Miami, Florida, USA. http://www.nhc.noaa.gov/data/tcr/AL182012_Sandy.pdf.

Blake, E. S., C. W. Landsea, and E. J. Gibney. "The Deadliest, Costliest, and Most Intense United States Tropical Cyclones from 1851 to 2010 (and Other Frequently Requested Hurricane Facts)." NOAA Technical Memorandum NWS NHC-6, 2011. http://www.nhc.noaa.gov/pdf/nws-nhc-6.pdf.

Chen, Q., L. Wang, and R. Tawes. "Hydrodynamic Response of Northeastern Gulf of Mexico to Hurricanes." *Estuaries and Coasts* 31 (1985): 1098–116.

Emanuel, K. *Divine Wind: The History and Science of Hurricanes.* Oxford: Oxford University Press, 2005.

Federal Emergency Management Agency. *Hurricane Ike in Texas and Louisiana: Mitigation Assessment Team Report, Building Performance Observations, Recommendations, and Technical Guidance (2009).* FEMA P-757. https://www.fema.gov/media-library/assets/documents/15498.

Garriott, E. B. "West Indian Hurricane of September 1–12, 1900." *Monthly Weather Review* 28 (1900): 371–78.

Harris, L. D. *Characteristics of the Hurricane Storm Surge.* US Weather Bureau, Technical Paper No. 48. 1963.

Irish, J. L., D. T. Resio, and J. J. Ratcliff. "The Influence of Storm Size on Hurricane Surge." *Journal of Physical Oceanography* 38 (2008): 2003–13.

Jordan, M. R., II, and C. A. Clayson. "Evaluating the Usefulness of a New Set of Hurricane Classification Indices." *Monthly Weather Review* 136 (2008): 5234–38.

Kates, R. W., C. E. Colten, S. Laska, and S. P. Leatherman. "Reconstruction of New Orleans after Hurricane Katrina: A Research Perspective." *Proceedings of the National Academy of Sciences of the United States of America* 103 (2006): 14653–60.

Keim, B., R. Muller, and G. Stone. "Spatiotemporal Patterns and Return Periods of Tropical Storm and Hurricane Strikes from Texas to Maine." *Journal of Climatology* 20 (2007): 3498–3509.

Kennedy, A. B., U. Gravois, B. C. Zachry, J. J. Westerink, M. E. Hope, J. C. Dietrich, M. D. Powell, A. T. Cox, R. A. Luettich Jr., and R. G. Dean (2011). "Origin of the Hurricane Ike Forerunner Surge." *Geophysical Research Letters* 38 (2011), L08608. doi:10.1029/2011GL047090.

Kessler, R. C., S. Galea, R. T. Jones, and H. A. Parker. "Mental Illness and Suicidality after Hurricane Katrina." *Bulletin of the World Health Organization* 84, no. 12 (2006): 930–39.

Kurian, N. P., N. Nirupama, M. Baba, and K. V. Thomas. "Coastal Flooding Due to Synoptic Scale, Meso-Scale and Remote Forcings." *Natural Hazards* 48 (2009): 259–73.

Lagmay, A. M. F., et al. "Devastating Storm Surges of Typhoon Haiyan." *International Journal of Disaster Risk Reduction* 11 (2015): 1–12.

McGee, B. D., B. B. Goree, R. W. Tollett, B. K. Woodward, and W. H. Kress. "Hurricane Rita Surge Data, Southwestern Louisiana and Southeastern Texas, September to November 2005." US Geological Survey, Data Series 220, 2013. pubs.usgs.gov/ds/2006/220/index.htm#desc.

National Oceanic and Atmospheric Administration. "Billion-Dollar Weather and Climate Disasters: Table of Events." National Centers for Environmental Information, 2015. http://www.ncdc.noaa.gov/billions/events.

Needham, H. F., and B. D. Keim. "Correlating Storm Surge Heights with Tropical Cyclone Winds at and before Landfall." *Earth Interactions* 8, no. 18 (2014): 1–26.

Nicholls, R. J. "Storm Surges in Coastal Areas." In *Natural Disaster Hot Spots Case Studies*, edited by M. Arnold, R. S. Chen, U. Deichmann, M. Dilley, A. L. Lerner-Lam, R. E. Pullen, and Z. Trohanis, 79–108. Washington, DC: International Bank for Reconstruction and Development, World Bank, 2006.

Rappaport, E. N, and J. Fernandez-Partagas. "The Deadliest Atlantic Tropical Cyclones, 1492–1994." NOAA Technical Memorandum NWS NHC-47. National Hurricane Center, 1995.

Smith, D. K. *Natural Disaster Reduction: How Meteorological and Hydrological Services Can Help*. Publication No. 722. Geneva, Switzerland: World Meteorological Organisation, 1989.

Theiss, M. "Hurricane Ivan, Pensacola Beach, FL." YouTube video of storm surge footage, 2:30–3:30, 2004. https://www.youtube.com/watch?v=o_uzqfhwc4k.

Welander, Pierre. "Numerical Prediction of Storm Surges." In *Advances in Geophysics*, vol. 8, edited by H. E. Landsberg and J. van Mieghem, 315–379. New York: Academic Press, 1961.

Galveston, TX

Population 50,180

6.89′ ABOVE SEA LEVEL

Reshaping Galveston Island after the 1900 Hurricane

Jodi Wright-Gidley

Life in Galveston at the end of the century was full, human, pleasant, and varied. The city possessed unusual charm, humor, maturity, and personality. Its climate and hazy sunshine produced a narcotic effect. Living was good. But Galveston existed on an edge, where nature's two worlds met. It was unsafe. This fragile, beautiful city . . . was caught and crushed."

—David G. McComb, *Galveston: A History*

Galveston was chartered in 1839[1] on a barrier island, and hurricanes have always been a big part of the city's history. After one hurricane in 1875, city leaders asked the state legislature to build a "break water." Galvestonians argued that because they paid one-eighth of the state's taxes, a proportionally large amount, the state should expend resources to protect the important port city, just as the state spent tax dollars to protect the western frontier. At that time, legislators were not willing to dedicate the funds. Many at the state capital in Austin believed that Galvestonians had helped create their own problems because they had been taking sand away from the beaches to fill in other areas. Some suggested the port be moved inland to let the Gulf "retake" Galveston Island.[2]

Although some saw Galveston as too risky for major investment, the town became a business center with railroad bridges and a wagon bridge linking it to mainland Texas and beyond. In 1890, the US Congress approved the Galveston Harbor Bill, making Galveston an official deep-water port. Jetties were built to concentrate and direct the ocean current, and dredging maintained the water depth to accommodate large ships. This federal action brought an increase in imports of about 55 percent, effectively saving the city at a time when railroad shipping over land was a serious threat to the port economy.[3] Galveston became home to more millionaires per capita than any other city in the United States. It was the most important port west of the Mississippi and the most sophisticated

Figure 4.1. The 1900 Galveston Hurricane destroyed roughly two-thirds of the city's buildings. (Courtesy of the Galveston County Museum, Galveston, Texas)

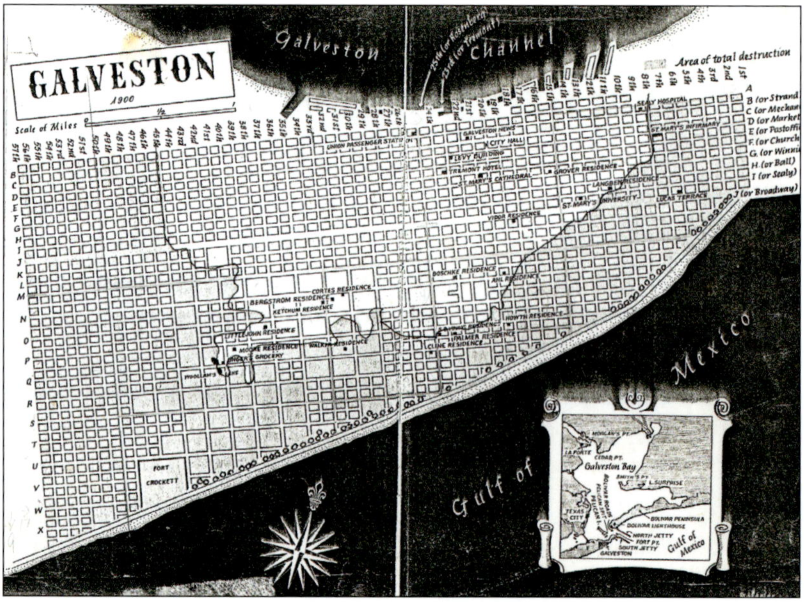

Figure 4.2. This map created after the 1900 Hurricane illustrates the extent of the storm's destruction on Galveston Island. Buildings outside the jagged U-shaped boundary were completely destroyed. (Courtesy of the Galveston County Museum, Galveston, Texas)

city in Texas. It had the state's first chamber of commerce, organized in 1845, and it was also the first city to have telephones and electricity. Its international atmosphere included a diverse population, numerous fancy restaurants, theaters, sporting events, and newspapers.[4]

However, after a massive hurricane hit the barrier island city on September 8, 1900, Galvestonians awoke to find about 6,000 of the city's 38,000 residents dead and 95 percent of the city damaged or destroyed. The debris pile was three miles long and two stories high. In the number of lives lost, Galveston's 1900 Storm remains the worst natural disaster in US history.

After the initial stages of recovery that involved meeting immediate human needs, burying the deceased, and cleaning up debris, Galvestonians began asking important questions: How can we rebuild better? What is the best method to protect the city from future storms? Who are the best engineers to talk to? Who will pay for the construction of some type of breakwater?

Constructing the Seawall

In the context of US history, Galveston was about to enter the Progressive Movement. With influence from powerful elite businessmen, the city's charter was rewritten, and new commissioners saw government as an ally not just for business interests but also for the good of the people. One of the first actions of the new government was to appoint a committee to select engineers to devise a plan for some type of breakwater. Engineers were solving problems all over the country. If this well-connected group with proven ideas could shape the environment in other places to the benefit of people, then they could do the same in Galveston.[6]

Three engineers—Brigadier General H. M. Robert, Alfred Noble, and H. C. Ripley—all of whom had previously worked on harbor and bridge projects in Galveston, proposed the construction of a 17-foot-tall concrete seawall and the raising of the city's grade. The project, eventually costing about $6 million, was funded by city and county coffers, as well as through bonds approved by an election with a 98 percent voter turnout.[7]

The proposal of Robert, Noble, and Ripley featured several traits designed to protect the city. At 17 feet, this seawall would be 1.3 feet higher than the storm surge of the 1900 Storm. A concave face would deflect waves back into the Gulf. After a bid solicitation process, J. M. O'Rourke

Figure 4.3. Engineers designed a seawall with a concave face to deflect waves. (Courtesy of the Galveston County Museum, Galveston, Texas, Zeva B. Edworthy Collection, donated by Judith Edworthy Wray)

Figure 4.4. The wall was built on wooden piles 40–44 feet long from East Texas pine, which anchored the structure into a deep layer of clay (Walden, "Raising Galveston," 12). (Courtesy of the Galveston County Museum, Galveston, Texas, Zeva B. Edworthy Collection, donated by Judith Edworthy Wray)

Figures 4.5 and 4.6. An apron of granite riprap about 27 feet long was placed in front of the wall to protect it from undermining (Walden, "Raising Galveston," 13). (Courtesy of the Galveston County Museum, Galveston, Texas, Zeva B. Edworthy Collection, donated by Judith Edworthy Wray)

Figure 4.7. The initial portion of the seawall wrapped around the eastern end of the island. (Courtesy of the Galveston County Museum, Galveston, Texas, Zeva B. Edworthy Collection, donated by Judith Edworthy Wray)

and Company received the contract to construct the seawall, and the cornerstone was laid in February 1903. The wall was built in alternating sections of 60 feet. One section was poured each day, and it took seven days for the concrete to dry.[8]

The initial portion, built between 1902 and 1904, was more than three miles long, and a year later the federal government completed a westward extension to protect Fort Crockett and Fort San Jacinto.[9] Additions in the twentieth century extended the existing seawall to more than 10 miles long, protecting about 30 square miles of the city where the majority of the population lived, or was predicted to live.

Raising the Grade

The next phase of the Galveston project involved raising 500 city blocks of land behind the seawall to the level of 17 feet and then gradually sloping it toward the bay.[10] The grade raising was accomplished by digging up sand from the seafloor in the port area and then discharging the muddy water through pipes into the city, where berms held the mud until it dried. A canal was built through town to accommodate dredge boats for the grade raising.

Figure 4.8. The grade-raising project included 500 city blocks. (Courtesy of the Galveston County Museum, Galveston, Texas, Zeva B. Edworthy Collection, donated by Judith Edworthy Wray)

Figure 4.9. Pipes carried sand dredged from the seafloor. (Courtesy of the Galveston County Museum, Galveston, Texas, Zeva B. Edworthy Collection, donated by Judith Edworthy Wray)

Figure 4.10. The right side of this photograph shows a dredge boat discharging muddy fill into a part of the city that had been prepared by placing the buildings on stilts. (Courtesy of the Galveston County Museum, Galveston, Texas, Zeva B. Edworthy Collection, donated by Judith Edworthy Wray)

Figure 4.11. St. Patrick's Catholic Church, which weighed 3,000 tons, took 35 days to elevate. (Courtesy of the Galveston County Museum, Galveston, Texas, Zeva B. Edworthy Collection, donated by Judith Edworthy Wray)

Before fill could be piped in, houses and other buildings in the affected area had to be raised to the new grade level. The nearer a house was to the seawall, the higher it had to be raised. The largest building raised was St. Patrick's Catholic Church, which weighed 3,000 tons. Using 700 jackscrews, contractors elevated the church five feet. Church services continued throughout the 35 days it took to complete the process.[11]

After the Projects

The port had been a driving force in Galveston's economy before the storm, and that continued to be the case afterward. Sailing vessels were used less frequently as huge steamships became more prevalent. These larger ships needed deeper water, which required dredging. Conveniently, dredging was a fundamental aspect of the grade-raising plan. The fill material pumped onto the island to raise the ground level was obtained from dredging the ocean floor around the ports.

Figures 4.12 and 4.13. This man is pointing to one of the numerous markers placed throughout town showing where the new ground level would be once the grade was raised. Buildings were raised at the owners' expense. Property that was not raised was surrounded by an earthen berm. The area was filled and the unraised property remained at the original, lower level. (Courtesy of the Galveston County Museum, Galveston, Texas, Zeva B. Edworthy Collection, donated by Judith Edworthy Wray)

Figure 4.14. Pipes carried muddy water into the city, where berms held the mud until it dried. (Courtesy of the Galveston County Museum, Galveston, Texas, Zeva B. Edworthy Collection, donated by Judith Edworthy Wray)

Figure 4.15. Raising was done in four-block sections. (Courtesy of the Galveston County Museum, Galveston, Texas, Zeva B. Edworthy Collection, donated by Judith Edworthy Wray)

Figure 4.16. Temporary wooden walkways and raised streetcar lines constantly changed, which made it confusing to maneuver in the city during this period. (Collection of the Galveston County Museum, Galveston, Texas, courtesy of Virginia Buck of Tishomingo, Oklahoma)

Figure 4.17. During the project, the grade-raising equipment became part of the city's landscape. (Courtesy of the Galveston County Museum, Galveston, Texas, Zeva B. Edworthy Collection, donated by Judith Edworthy Wray)

Figures 4.18 and 4.19. A neighborhood before and after the grade raising. (Courtesy of the Galveston County Museum, Galveston, Texas, Zeva B. Edworthy Collection, donated by Judith Edworthy Wray)

Figure 4.20. After the first section of seawall was completed in 1904, the beach area underwent a boom of new construction to entice tourists to the beach. Tourism was a significant focus of Galveston's economic recovery after the 1900 Storm. (Courtesy of the Galveston County Museum, Galveston, Texas, Zeva B. Edworthy Collection, donated by Judith Edworthy Wray)

Figure 4.21. Between 1906 and 1914, about 50,000 immigrants came through Galveston, some as part of the Jewish "Galveston Movement" (Manaster, "Galveston Movement"). Galveston became a significant port of entry for immigrants when Ellis Island began to place restrictions. (Courtesy of the Galveston County Museum, Galveston, Texas, Zeva B. Edworthy Collection, donated by Judith Edworthy Wray)

Figure 4.22. As World War I began, Galveston was the leading cotton exporter in the world. (Collection of the Galveston County Museum, Galveston, Texas, courtesy of Virginia Buck of Tishomingo, Oklahoma)

Figure 4.23. Galveston, home of the first medical school in Texas, continued its focus on medical education and research after the grade-raising projects. When the state decided to fund a medical school, Galveston was thought to be an ideal location because immigrants were believed to be bringing in foreign illnesses that needed to be studied and cured before they spread throughout Texas (McComb, ***Galveston***, 98). (Courtesy of the Galveston County Museum, Galveston, Texas, Zeva B. Edworthy Collection, donated by Judith Edworthy Wray)

Galveston followed the success of the seawall and grade-raising projects with the construction of a new causeway linking Galveston Island to the Texas mainland. The new causeway opened in 1912 with lanes for railcars, automobiles, wagons, and pedestrians. A few years later, the Galveston-Houston Interurban Rail also crossed the causeway, allowing the numbers of people visiting Galveston to steadily increase through the twentieth century.[12]

These major engineering efforts did not go untested. Hurricanes again struck the island in 1909 and 1915. The hurricane in 1915 was even more powerful than the 1900 Storm. The fill material pumped in for the grade raising was shifty, leaving damaged foundations and sunken buildings.

Figure 4.24. A new causeway opened in 1912. (Courtesy of the Galveston County Museum, Galveston, Texas, Zeva B. Edworthy Collection, donated by Judith Edworthy Wray)

However, only eight lives were lost in Galveston within the area protected by the seawall, as opposed to the 6,000 who had perished in the 1900 Storm before the seawall was built.[13]

> **Its struggle for survival against nature through the application of technology represents the strongest tradition of Western civilization. Galveston's response to the great storm of 1900 was its finest hour, and demonstrated that rationality and determination can prevail. This is the lesson that Galveston teaches all visitors who come to the edge of time, stand on the seawall, and gaze in wonder upon the vastness of the sea.**
>
> **—David G. McComb, *Galveston: A History***

Acknowledgments

The author would like to recognize Jennifer Marines, whose contributions made this chapter possible.

Notes

1. David G. McComb, *Galveston: A History* (Austin: University of Texas Press, 1986), 43.
2. Ibid., 30.
3. Ibid., 60–61.
4. Ibid., 104–5, 118.
5. Don Walden, "Raising Galveston," *American Heritage of Invention and Technology*, Winter 1990, 10.
6. McComb, *Galveston*, 137.
7. Ibid., 138–39.
8. Ibid., 139.
9. Ibid., 140.
10. "The Relocation of Public Service Systems during the Grade Raising of Galveston, Tex.," *Engineering Record* 54, no. 11 (September 15, 1906): 300.
11. McComb, *Galveston*, 142.
12. Ibid., 143, 145.
13. Ibid., 145, 148.

Bibliography

Beasley, Ellen, and Stephen Fox. *Galveston Architecture Guidebook*. Houston: Rice University Press, 1996.

Burka, Paul. "Grande Dame of the Gulf." *Texas Monthly*, December 1983. Accessed November 23, 2016. http://www.texasmonthly.com/articles/grande-dame-of-the-gulf-2/.

Eisenhour, Virginia. *Galveston: A Different Place; A History and Guide*. Galveston, TX: self-published, 2003.

Fox, Stephen. "Broadway, Galveston, Texas." In *The Grand American Avenue: 1850–1920*, edited by Jan Cigliano and Landau Sarah Bradford, 207–30. San Francisco: Pomegranate Artbooks, 1994.

Galveston County Historical Commission. Resource and state marker files. Galveston County Historical Museum, 2219 Market Street, Galveston, TX.

Hanna, James S. *What Life Was Like When I Was a Kid*. San Antonio, TX: Naylor, 1973.

Kelso, Margy. *A Glance Back: The First Century of the Galveston Country Club*. Galveston, TX: Galveston County Club, 1998.

Kessler, Jimmy. *Henry Cohen: The Life of a Frontier Rabbi*. Austin, TX: Eakin Press, 1997.

Manaster, Jane. "Galveston Movement." *Handbook of Texas Online*. Texas State Historical Association. Accessed July 9, 2016. http://www.tshaonline.org/handbook/online/articles/umg01.

McComb, David G. *Galveston: A History*. Austin: University of Texas Press, 1986.
"Raising Large Brick Buildings in Galveston, Texas." *Engineering Record* 59, no. 14 (April 3, 1909).
Scardino, Barrie, and Drexel Turner. *Clayton's Galveston: The Architecture of Nicholas J. Clayton and His Contemporaries*. College Station: Texas A&M University Press, 2000.
Turner, Elizabeth Hayes. *Women, Culture, and Community: Religion and Reform in Galveston, 1880–1920*. New York: Oxford University Press, 1997.
Wright-Gidley, Jodi, and Jennifer Marines. *Galveston: A City on Stilts*. Charleston, SC: Arcadia Publishing, 2008.

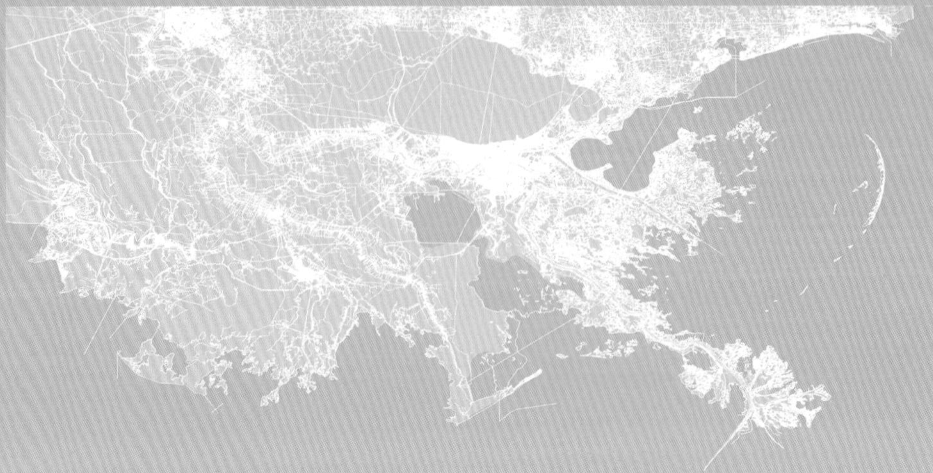

South Louisiana

MSA Population 1,262,888

1' BELOW SEA LEVEL

Resilient Housing Lessons from Katrina

Claudette Hanks Reichel

Hindsight Is 20/20 . . . Foresight Is Priceless

Hurricanes and flooding have been part of the way of life in Louisiana throughout its history. In fact, the founding of New Orleans was postponed for two years because of flooding. Some say that should have been a clue! Yet the vital economic benefits of building and living at the mouth of the mighty Mississippi outweighed the risk. Now, it's a cultural treasure as well.

Figure. 5.1. Louisiana—living with natural hazards as a vital national resource. (Photo by Claudette Hanks Reichel)

Likewise, coastal Louisiana is a vital resource for the entire nation, ranking second in the nation in energy production. Shrimp and oysters are more plentiful than in any other coastal area, and freshwater fisheries lead the nation in catch. Furthermore, Louisiana coastal communities and housing are not predominantly resorts and vacation homes, but the homes of workers and residents who support and provide these crucial benefits.[1]

Living with natural hazards shaped a relatively resilient traditional housing stock of raised homes on piers with "flow-through" building systems of wood lumber framing, flooring, and siding, no insulation, and plaster interior finishes that could readily dry and be restored after inundation. As housing development and design evolved after World War II in response to air conditioning, the energy crisis of the 1970s, and population growth and trends, the traditional Louisiana housing vernacular and its inherent resilience gave way to other growing priorities of modern construction and development practices: price, expectations of comfort, energy costs, style and market trends, and new technologies. The dominant housing stock evolved toward slab-on-grade homes with fibrous insulation-filled walls, moisture-sensitive materials, wall-to-wall carpeting and sheet-vinyl flooring, vinyl wallpaper, central air conditioning, stapled sheathing, and flimsy three-tab shingle roofing.

Amid rising disaster losses and public costs, the American Association of Housing Educators (now HERA) and the Extension Disaster Education Network (EDEN) hosted a national "Breaking the Housing Disaster Cycle" conference in New Orleans in 1997 to explore policy, structural, and behavioral mitigation strategies. Years before, scientists had developed models depicting the potential impacts of a category 3 storm on New Orleans. Needless to say, the "housing disaster cycle" not only continued, but mushroomed.

At the start of the new millennium, the Louisiana Cooperative Extension Service, an educational outreach arm of the Louisiana State University AgCenter, began an initiative to create the Louisiana House (LaHouse) Resource Center with a vision of shaping the future for Louisiana living. It set out to address national housing issues and state challenges associated with disaster costs, energy costs, and health and economic vitality in a region vulnerable to hurricanes, floods, termites, decay, mold, and pollution.

Then in 2005, the predicted models became reality when impacts from Hurricanes Katrina (east Louisiana) and Rita (west Louisiana) hit the

Figure. 5.2. LaHouse is a showcase of solutions and an educational outreach program for high-performance homes in the Gulf Region. (LSU AgCenter)

coast just three weeks apart. The record-shattering losses from this disaster gave new, tragic meaning and focus to the LaHouse adage "As we shape our homes . . . we shape our future." It took not months but years to recover from damage of this magnitude to homes and to the people who lived in them.

Why Did It Take So Long?

The aftermath of the dual Katrina/Rita disaster was unprecedented in the United States: 1,833 deaths,[2] 182,000 housing units lost, more than 440,000 households displaced,[3] 31 percent of the Louisiana housing stock damaged, over 113.5 million cubic yards of debris,[4] 81,000 businesses affected, and historical legacies and cultures threatened.

Behind those grim numbers is the impact on people. The work, the time, the cost, and the toll on families were profound beyond words. The ripple effect impacted everyone and the economy. Yet a year later (several years in many areas), scenes of damaged homes and neighborhoods

Figure. 5.3. Hurricanes Katrina and Rita left behind more than 182,000 destroyed housing units. (FEMA)

Figure. 5.4. Sixty million cubic yards of debris lined streets and filled lots, awaiting the monumental task of disposal. (LSU AgCenter)

Figure. 5.5. An example of the ordeal Katrina evacuees faced when allowed to return home. (LSU AgCenter)

Figure. 5.6. Aftermath of Hurricane Rita in coastal west Louisiana. (LSU AgCenter)

remained. Why did it take so long? There were many reasons and many targets of blame. Many of the contributing factors listed below were outside prior experience and thus not anticipated or included in the current disaster response systems.

- In terms of damage, Katrina was the most massive disaster ever to occur in the United States, surpassing every government entity's plan and capacity to manage. Often-overlooked Rita caused more wind damage, but total losses and attention to recovery were dwarfed by Katrina.
- As a result, there was fumbling at *every* level—federal, state, and local governments and agencies. Disrupted communications, utilities, transportation, local emergency and police forces, medical services, and impacted staff complicated response and recovery.
- Flooding lasted weeks, not days. A large population was displaced for extended periods. Hundreds of thousands of evacuees became refugees; many became homeless.
- Families and businesses lost their sources of revenue for long periods, some entirely.
- Political turf battles and blaming ensued, hampering progress.
- Levees built for protection became the cause of destruction. Heated debates ensued: What should be done? How much should be spent? Who should pay? Should rebuilding even be allowed in a city below sea level?
- Lack of housing meant there were no places to house workers and volunteers to help recover.

Too Little, Too Slow

The array of financial assistance sources for restoring homes was grossly outmatched by the disaster. Contrary to popular belief, housing assistance from the Federal Emergency Management Agency (FEMA) is statutorily limited to *temporary* housing only—giving birth to vast and scorned "FEMA trailer" neighborhoods and communities.

Flood insurance offered only a fraction of households' rebuilding needs. Many homeowners had no flood insurance, often because they

Figure. 5.7. A "gutted" home in New Orleans a year after the storm. (LSU AgCenter)

had no mortgage that would require it, or their homes were not in flood zones because of old flood maps or "protections" such as levees and pump systems (which failed). Homeowners' insurance does not cover flood damage and usually excludes mold remediation. Disputes abounded as to which damages were due to wind and which were due to flooding, and thus not covered.

It took 10 months to scale political hurdles and secure congressional authorization for federal disaster assistance for homeowners. It was nearly two years before funds began to reach homeowners through the Road Home Program. The complexity and difficulties in designing and administering such a massive and untested housing disaster assistance program resulted in what was deemed a "long, winding road home full of potholes." Eventually, 113,000 homeowners received a total of $9 billion to bridge the gap between insurance and rebuilding cost limits set by the

Figure. 5.8. Long-term wetness resulted in massive mold growth before restoration could begin after Katrina, and mold remediation is typically not covered by homeowners' insurance. (LSU AgCenter)

program. The funding was too little and too slow, and thus too late for many of the Katrina homeless and long displaced.

Too Much, Too Fast!

Recovery was also hampered by an explosion of competing or overlapping forums, committees, and initiatives, albeit well intentioned. There was a battle among regional plans designed by experts and community processes, which were repeatedly resisted or rejected by constituents, and the complexity of the task.

As water receded, mold grew fast and thick, enveloping homes and furnishings. Conflicting cleanup guidelines and misinformation multiplied along with the mold. Thousands of homeowners and volunteers had to tackle the mold cleanup themselves, subjecting themselves to the health risks of massive mold exposure, flood contaminants, lead-based paint, debris hazards, and more. An influx of alternative and expensive remediation services bombarded homeowners who had the capacity to pay.

Hindsight Is 20/20

Code Complications

To prevent an exodus of property insurers, Louisiana rapidly enacted a statewide uniform residential construction code, based on the latest International Residential Code (IRC), and a state code council. Louisiana had previously had a patchwork of various, typically long-outdated residential codes selected by local jurisdictions. Many rural areas and some parishes had no building codes other than flood ordinances required by the National Flood Insurance Program (NFIP), so they had no building permit process, officials, or inspectors.

None of the preexisting codes included wind code provisions. Emergency wind and flood provisions went into effect immediately for 11 coastal parishes and for the rest of the state a year later, according to the IRC wind speed maps. The IRC uses NFIP standards for building elevations in flood zones according to current maps, but FEMA's poststorm "flood advisory" higher elevation levels were required if public money was used in rebuilding.

This rapid code adoption kept homeowners' insurance available but posed an extremely steep learning curve for contractors, and a nearly impossible challenge for most jurisdictions to enforce new codes, particularly where complex wind provisions applied. There was a severe shortage of code officials, no inspectors certified by the International Code Council (ICC), and few design professionals familiar with residential wood-frame, high-wind design. Third-party inspectors were scarce. Architects and engineers could legally verify code compliance, but liability insurance ramifications and costs made this option generally unavailable. Funding for the staffing and training of building permit departments was not provided until two years after the codes were enacted. Because of these problems, coupled with the enormous demand for rebuilding permits, backlogs grew and some areas had to impose moratoriums.

Rebuilding Obstacles

An instant, gigantic housing demand coincided with a severe skilled-labor shortage, producing intense wage competition, overloaded trades, and an influx of migrant workers (with language barriers and no housing for them). Demand and disrupted distribution chains rapidly resulted in building material shortages and price hikes. Estimating construction costs was like aiming at a moving target. Appraisals came in below cost, reducing loan limit and qualifying. Insurance rates spiked and utilities imposed surcharges for their repair expenses.

Influx

Sadly, unlicensed contractors swooped into the state and preyed on disaster victims desperate to restore their homes and lives. On the other hand, a cornucopia of housing and building alternatives arrived to tap this large, albeit temporary, new market. Large production builders developed areas outside New Orleans; only one remains. Manufactured and modular homes from established producers attempted to fill the need with homes reinforced for wind zones, but projects were constrained by access limitations in the city and by other logistics. Expandable "Katrina Cottage" kits made a media splash as a better alternative to FEMA trailers, but they could not be funded by FEMA. Factory assembly proved too difficult at the time, community resistance mounted, and few households with the

Figure. 5.9. Licensed contractors were overwhelmed. A deluge of unlicensed contractors flocked to disaster areas and preyed on desperate storm victims. (LSU AgCenter)

capacity to build chose the Katrina Cottage option, forming a negative stigma. Known as the "Losing Everything I Ever Owned Cottage," the kits became more popular for recreational "camps."

Alternative steel-framing and concrete building systems (including the insulating concrete form [ICF] and insulated sandwich panel system [ISPS]) touted their flood, wind, and termite resistance. However, costs, norms, and trade skills constrained their production to a small niche and few homes. ICF building continues in a small, high-end market niche.

Panelized building systems, such as structural insulated panels (SIPs), provided fast construction of energy-efficient homes with less-skilled labor. A SIP modular housing plant was launched and produced affordable, efficient, and wind-resistant homes that were transported to sites and quickly completed on raised foundations above flood risk. The plant could not sustain enough business over the years after recovery to remain

Figure. 5.10. Structural insulated panel (SIP) system. (LSU AgCenter)

profitable and has since closed. Site-built SIP building continues in niche markets, including the high-profile "Make It Right" initiative launched by actor Brad Pitt.

How-to Resources—Better Late Than Never

The immense challenges of the post-Katrina/Rita housing recovery spawned new information resources, education and training programs, and technologies that helped scale the learning curve, accelerate rebuilding progress, and produce more resilient housing. Along with the new uniform building code, the new resources aimed to raise the bar of quality and other home-performance benefits including durability, energy efficiency, and health. New Orleans in particular embraced the green building movement among other "wipe the slate clean and re-create it better" recovery initiatives (concerning education, government, and other sectors), although the goal was certainly not universal and not always successful.

Since Katrina, improved building design, methods, products, and technologies that cost-effectively reduce water intrusion and increase strength have emerged. Particularly helpful resources were developed and are now available to all who live and build on the edge, including the following:

- Free, builder-friendly, illustrated prescriptive *WFCM High Wind Guides* (by wind design speed) based on the *Wood Frame Construction Manual* standard (www.awc.org) and the detailed *ICC 600 Standard for Residential Construction in High-Wind Regions* (www.iccsafe.org)
- Lower-cost residential e-engineering services developed as a hybrid of engineered and prescriptive design standards
- Layman-friendly, illustrated FEMA publications, particularly FEMA P-499, *Home Builder's Guide to Coastal Construction* series (revised 2010); FEMA P-804, *Wind Retrofit Guide for Residential Buildings* (2010); FEMA P-85, *Protecting Manufactured Homes from Floods and Other Hazards* (2009); and FEMA P-550, *Recommended Residential Construction for Coastal Areas: Building on Strong and Safe Foundations* (2009), all free downloads from www.fema.gov
- Code-plus, hazard-resistant home-building guides, certification and training programs, consumer education, and research reports

online, including the "Fortified for Safer Living" program of the Insurance Institute for Business and Home Safety (IBHS) at www.disastersafety.org and the *Blueprint for Safety* building guide of the Federal Alliance for Safe Homes (FLASH) at www.flash.org

- Residential building science research findings made accessible through guides, publications, case studies (including post-Katrina prototype projects), and marketing tools on high-performance, durable new construction and retrofit from the US Department of Energy's (DOE) online Building America Solution Center (basc.pnnl.gov) and from Building Science Corporation's large searchable collection of free online documents (buildingscience.com).
- A growing collection developed by the US Department of Housing and Urban Development (HUD):

  The PD&R Disaster Response Toolkit, available from HUD USER online (www.huduser.gov) or by calling (800) 245–2691

  HUD's new OLHCHH Disaster Recovery Toolkit, which gives new guidance resources for consumers, volunteers, workers, and stakeholders and includes short videos and fact sheets

  The detailed *Rebuild Healthy Homes: Guide to Post-Disaster Restoration for a Safe and Healthy Home* (2015), available both as a pdf publication at www.hud.gov/healthyhomes and as a free mobile app from Apple and Android app stores

Foresight Is Priceless

Hindsight is easy and clear, like 20/20 vision, to those who look. Foresight, on the other hand, is hard to materialize in the real world, but its rewards would be priceless! Imagine resilient homes that could withstand most natural hazards. Then families could return home soon after a hazard ended, clean and restore their homes quickly and inexpensively, and rapidly resume their normal lives and businesses. Billions of tax dollars would be saved for other public needs. Unimaginable suffering would be averted. The list of benefits does not stop there.

The knowledge and technology to produce truly resilient, high-performance housing is available and feasible, even within the typical

Figure. 5.11. Green Dream 1, a prototype resilient, high-performance home. (LSU AgCenter)

Figure. 5.12. Green Dream 2, a prototype resilient, high-performance home. (LSU AgCenter)

Figure. 5.13. Volunteers helped build the Green Dream prototype homes and many others. (LSU AgCenter)

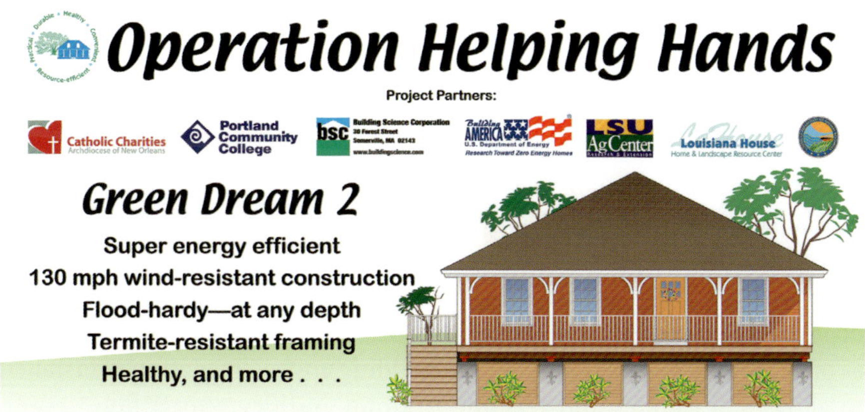

Figure. 5.14. Prototype homes integrate resilience with high efficiency and healthy home qualities. (LSU AgCenter)

constraints of affordable, wood-frame, site-built construction using local contractors and materials. To demonstrate and analyze this potential, two prototype houses were built in New Orleans in 2006 by the New Orleans Catholic Charities in partnership with the Building Science Corporation (BSC), the DOE Building America program, and the LaHouse Resource Center. The prototypes, locally dubbed Green Dream (GD) Homes 1 and 2, replaced the destroyed homes of two limited-resource households in the devastated Gentilly neighborhood. GD2 housed a family of eight.

The modest homes are elevated, flood-hardy, 130 mph wind-resistant, termite-resistant, and energy-efficient wood-frame houses designed by BSC and built within the $150,000 limit of the Road Home grant program (with some volunteer labor and material donations). Their attributes were achieved as an integrated system tailored to the local hot, humid, rainy climate and natural hazards, with recognition of local skills, materials, and home style norms.

Flood-Hardy Home Solutions

The houses are elevated two feet above the required base flood elevation (BFE), so they are five feet above grade, providing a cushion of safety and lower flood insurance premiums. Foundations are piers on continuous footings, producing stability and no impact on the floodplain or neighbors. BFE reflects a 1 percent per year probability of flood risk based on levee protection. If the levees or pumps ever failed again or if they were overtopped by a stronger storm surge, flood levels could repeat Katrina's outcomes of water 8–12 feet deep. Therefore, these homes are designed so flooding at that level would do little or no damage, with drainable, dryable wall and floor assemblies.

Wall and floor framing consist entirely of flood- and termite-resistant materials: borate pressure-treated solid lumber and treated plywood sheathing with no use of oriented strand board (OSB) or laminated beams. Walls are insulated with nonabsorbent closed-cell foam insulation at or beyond R-values mandated by building codes. Insulation is installed to allow wall cavities and framing to drain and dry after a flood event. GD1 has 2.5 inches of closed-cell spray foam within wall cavities, creating a partial fill. The foam also creates an airtight building enclosure and adds structural load capacity. GD2 has 2-inch, foil-faced, rigid foam-board insulation outside the structural sheathing, leaving wall cavities empty for optimal drainage and drying capacity.

Figure. 5.15. This model illustrates a washable, drainable, dryable "flood-hardy" building assembly that was demonstrated in the Green Dream 2 house. (Photo by Claudette Hanks Reichel)

Figure. 5.16. The prototype homes use only flood- and termite-resistant structural materials. (LSU AgCenter)

Figure. 5.17. GD2 flood-hardy walls have exterior closed-cell, rigid foam-board insulation and empty wall cavities. (LSU AgCenter)

Figure. 5.18. Closed-cell spray-foam insulation under floor joists, sealed airtight, is flood resilient and prevents subfloor moisture problems. (LSU AgCenter)

Subfloors are also insulated with closed-cell foam insulation to not only withstand floods but also prevent floor moisture problems common in air-conditioned homes in a warm, humid climate. The moisture-related issues are typically worsened by traditional fibrous subfloor insulation because of the long summer inward water vapor drive. One of the model houses has fire-rated, foil-faced, rigid foam boards encasing floor joists, carefully taped and sealed to create an airtight, vapor-barrier insulation system. After a flood, strips of foam board can be cut out to drain and then taped back into place. The other house has closed-cell spray foam between floor joists and at the rim, also producing an airtight, vapor-barrier subfloor insulation system.

Wall interiors are finished with paperless, fiberglass mat–faced gypsum drywall with a moisture-resistant core. The product is a FEMA-designated flood damage–resistant material. It has no paper facing and provides no food for mold or termites. Drywall is finished with latex paint for maximum water vapor permeability to allow drying of moisture in walls through the drywall and finish to the air-conditioned interior.

Drywall gaps were left behind the molding in these two prototype homes so that after a flood, the trim can be removed and the wall cavities flushed to clean and sanitize, drained, and allowed to dry, avoiding the need to gut the walls and replace insulation and drywall (saltwater-affected electrical wiring would need replacement). This could allow families to avoid great delays, ordeal, and expense after a flood and to restore their homes and lives much sooner.

Ceramic tile flooring can survive flooding and be restored. Prefinished fiber cement siding and trim is flood hardy, termite resistant, strong, and low maintenance.

A major challenge and lesson learned was the crucial importance of worker training and close oversight with new and nonstandard methods. Although both flood-hardy systems remain viable, using closed-cell spray foam reduced the learning curve and time required. The Building Science Corporation recently devised a "new, improved," hybrid flood-hardy building system. It uses XPS foam sheathing in place of wood sheathing plus a minimum of two-inch-thick, closed-cell (two-pound density) spray foam in the wall cavity, which provides the structural load-racking resistance.[5]

The flood-hardy concept can also be applied to the restoration of existing flooded homes, also known as "wet floodproofing." A washable, drainable, dryable restoration that omits the need to gut and replace wallboard, insulation, and sheathing could greatly reduce the expense, ordeal, and time required for homeowners to return home and resume their lives. Each flood-hardy restoration method has different advantages, risks, and considerations that should be weighed. Historical homes may also have restrictions to preserve original materials and ensure that changes, such as spray-foam installation, are reversible.

Hurricane-Hardy Home Solutions

Construction plans for the two prototype homes were detailed according to the 130 mph prescriptive wind standard from the *Wood Frame Construction Manual*, a notch beyond code for a cushion of safety. Additional details were included to prevent wind-driven water intrusion, a major source of storm damage.

The roof, which is most commonly damaged during windstorms, is the top priority. Both houses have treated plywood roof decking securely attached to rafters with ring shank nails at six-inch spacing for higher pullout resistance (a low-cost upgrade). Peel-and-stick membrane roofing underlayment provides a robust secondary moisture barrier in the event of shingle loss. Roof decks for both GD houses are fully covered with the adhesive membrane. Lower-cost alternatives include taping only the seams with roof-approved tape and properly fastening tear-resistant synthetic roofing underlayment.

The roofing was UL 2390 Class H, tested to withstand 150 mph winds, and UL Class 4 hail-resistant composition shingles. Both roofs were installed according to high-wind manufacturer instructions. Crucial elements included a dedicated starter strip (*not* trimmed shingles) and six nails per shingle in specified locations.

The larger GD2 house has a simple hip roof design with moderate slope, which is inherently aerodynamic and less vulnerable to wind damage. In both houses, roof overhangs do not extend beyond two feet, except for porches with columns secured with hurricane hardware to resist uplift forces.

Hurricane hardware (metal connectors) was detailed on the plans and installed to provide a continuous load path from the roof ridge to the foundation and to resist higher wind loads at corners and openings. This included properly spaced anchor bolts with three-inch washers, stud-to-plate connectors, post straps, corner hold-downs, and wrap-over rafter/truss straps for lower failure risk as lumber ages.

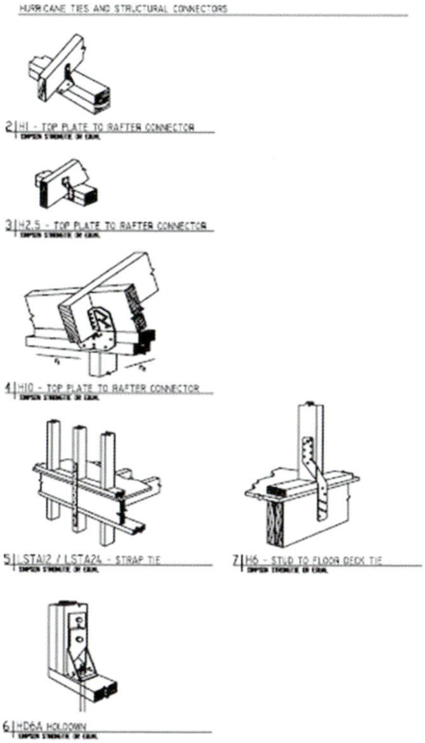

Figure. 5.19. Construction plans detailed hurricane hardware connections for 130 mph wind load. (LSU AgCenter)

Figure. 5.20. Hurricane connectors included wrap-over truss straps as a best practice. (LSU AgCenter)

Continuous structural sheathing of exterior walls and the roof resists racking, otherwise known as shear forces. Sheathing extends over the top and bottom plates. Blocking was added at seams so all edges of sheathing are nailed to framing.

Impact-rated windows and doors were chosen to provide protection from windborne debris at a lower cost than operable hurricane shutters. They have a clear membrane within the glass that prevents broken glass from resulting in a large "hole" that could admit enough wind to amplify stresses on the structure and cause structural failure. Although removable storm panels are less expensive, they require storage and difficult prestorm installation on a ladder.

Solutions to Keep It Dry

Water intrusion is a year-round durability issue in this climate, and an intensified risk during storms. Proper layering and integration of weather barriers and flashing of openings to provide an effective drainage plane behind siding is crucial, yet it is often lacking or flawed in typical construc-

Figure. 5.21. Windowsill flashing includes crucial corner protection. (LSU AgCenter)

tion. Drawings of installation steps and worker training ensured correct installation and lasting protection.

Windows have adhesive sill flashing systems with corner guards. Flashing tape covered window side flanges after housewrap and window installation, and then the top flange was flashed. The bottom flange was not taped to allow window unit leaks to drain to the exterior. Gaps between the window and framing were filled on the interior side with low-expansion foam sealant to seal air and prevent wind-driven water leaks. Similar flashing integration was installed to prevent leaks at doors, exhaust dampers, and other wall penetrations.

GD1 (with spray-foam insulation in wall cavities) has tear-resistant, nonperforated housewrap properly installed with cap nails over the plywood sheathing. Vertical furring strips over the housewrap create a vented "rain screen" space behind the siding. Insect screen material was wrapped

Figure. 5.22. The bottom flanges of windows are ***not*** taped, allowing drainage of unit leaks to the outside. (LSU AgCenter)

Figure. 5.23. With an exterior insulation system, furring strips provide both rain screen and nail base for secure siding installation. (LSU AgCenter)

under the bottom of the furring strips to exclude insects from the drainage space.

GD2 (with exterior rigid-foam insulation) has housewrap over the plywood sheathing, then the rigid-foam insulation over the housewrap. Vertical one-by-four furring strips were installed on the foam panels with long screws installed through the foam into the framing, with a screen wrapped around the bottom to act as an insect excluder. Window wells were trimmed out and the prefinished fiber cement siding secured through furring strips into the framing.

Termite Control Solutions

The Formosan subterranean termite, prevalent in New Orleans and spreading throughout the South, is the most destructive insect on Earth. It can cause major structural damage within only one year of infestation. A termite-damaged house can be weakened, so resistance to wood-destroying insects is crucial to hurricane and flood resistance.

Figure. 5.24. Structural framing with borate pressure-treated lumber provides protection from decay and highly destructive Formosan subterranean termites. (LSU AgCenter)

The GD houses invested in several lines of termite defense beyond the minimum code requirement of soil treatment. Metal termite barriers between the foundation and wood framing extend beyond the piers and force termites to reveal themselves from hidden pathways inside the piers. Moisture attracts termites, so best practices for moisture control are important. For added protection, structural lumber was borate pressure treated, and treated plywood was used. Borates are an effective yet safe and environmentally friendly protective treatment. They are also less corrosive to fasteners than copper-based treatments, which are necessary for exposed outdoor wood uses.

Additional Durability Solutions

Long-lasting, low-maintenance materials and equipment increase durability and long-term affordability. GD homes have foundations designed for the soil type, 30-year-warranty roofing, 10-year window frames with

20-year glass, long-lasting types of siding and flooring, HVAC equipment, and appliances with long warranties.

Energy-Saving and Comfort Solutions

Long-term affordability also requires climate-appropriate energy efficiency to achieve a comfortable and healthy living space at a low monthly cost. A house is a system. In order to perform well and avoid problems that can erode durability or indoor air quality, it must be built with an understanding of basic building science principles of air, heat, and moisture dynamics.

The GD homes have airtight, moisture-managed building enclosures with effective insulation systems; low-e Energy Star, impact-rated windows; and insulated doors. All central air ductwork is within conditioned space in unvented, semiconditioned attics with open-cell spray foam under the roof decking. A relatively high-efficiency (15.5 and 16 SEER) air source heat pump was installed with a supply-only mechanical ventilation system to provide controlled fresh air (a central fan integrated with

Figure. 5.25. HVAC unit and ducts entirely within conditioned space via the foam-sealed, semiconditioned attic. The sealed attic also omits the risk of wind-driven rain intrusion. (LSU AgCenter)

motorized flow control), and a supplemental Energy Star dehumidifier to maintain comfort and a healthy indoor humidity level when the air conditioner does not run enough to meet the latent load (humidity), a likely occurrence during spring and fall in efficient homes. The homes also have Energy Star appliances and efficient compact fluorescent lighting. The Home Energy Rating System (HERS) index measures energy efficiency. A score of HERS 100 represents a 2006 energy code–compliant house. The smaller the index, the closer to zero energy. GD1 achieved a score of HERS 64; GD2 achieved HERS 56.

These energy-saving features still exceed the Louisiana residential energy code requirements in place in 2018. However, as technologies improve, higher-efficiency equipment and LED lighting are now cost-effective and advantageous.

Showcase of Solutions

The LaHouse Resource Center was in midconstruction when Katrina and Rita devastated the state. It was ironically at the ideal stage to serve as a ready "showcase of solutions," as dubbed by a New Orleans reporter. It was strategically designed and constructed to exhibit four high-performance

Figure. 5.26. LaHouse paused construction after Katrina to fully exhibit the resilient features of its four building systems. (LSU AgCenter)

building and foundation systems with Fortified for Safer Living hurricane- and flood-resistant features, flood-hardy alternatives, moisture control details, and termite lines of defense, along with high energy efficiency, indoor air quality, and universal design. The building systems include enhanced two-by-four wood framing, advanced framing, SIP, and ICF.

Foresight Was Indeed Priceless!

LaHouse was left in that midconstruction state for two years following the storms and was toured by thousands. It was then completed in 2008 with cutaways, displays, point-of-feature signage, and literature. The house remains on exhibit as an educational resource open to the public.

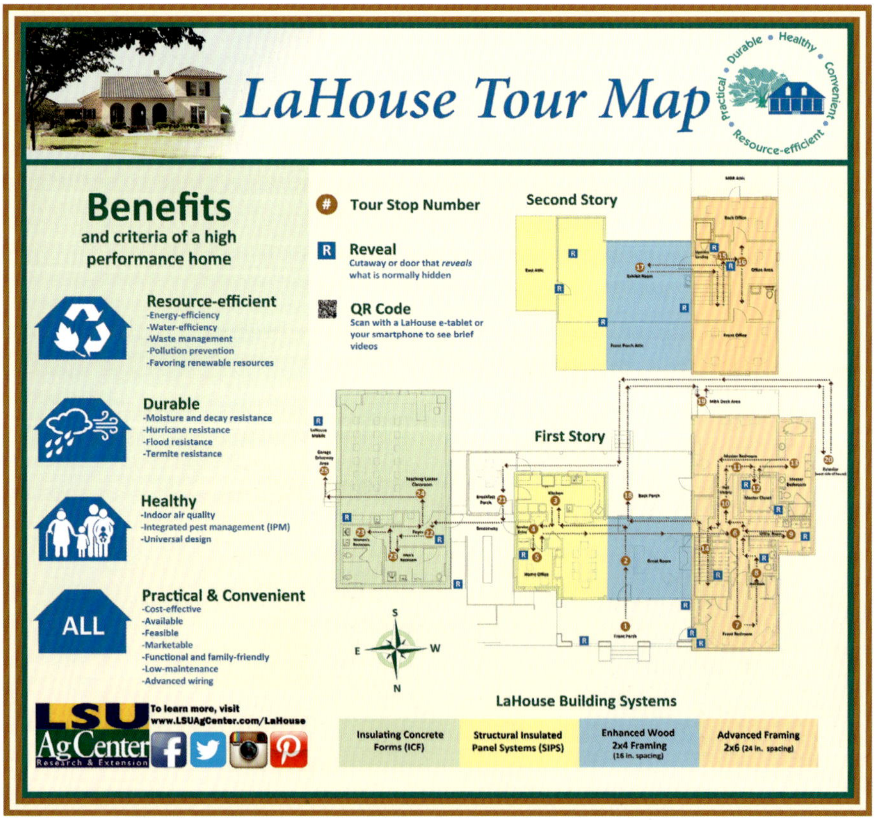

Figure. 5.27. LaHouse is an educational public service, exhibiting a range of resilient housing solutions for living on the edge. (LSU AgCenter)

You can see and learn more at www.lsuagcenter.com/LaHouse, watch short videos about each of its building systems and foundations at www.youtube.com/mylahouse, and tour in person.

Conclusion

My own wish and motive in contributing this chapter is my fervent hope that Louisiana's tragic hindsight will become the nation's foresight. We have experienced firsthand that as we shape our homes, we *truly* shape our future.

Notes

1. *A Coastal User's Guide to the Louisiana Coastal Resources Program*, Louisiana Department of Natural Resources Office of Coastal Management, January 2015, http://data.dnr.louisiana.gov/LCP/LCPHANDBOOK/FinalUsersGuide.pdf.

2. "Facts for Features: Hurricane Katrina 10th Anniversary: August 29, 2015," US Census Bureau, Release Number CB15-FF.16, July 29, 2015, accessed August 2, 2016, http://www.census.gov/newsroom/facts-for-features/2015/cb15-ff16.html.

3. *The Gulf Coast: Economic Impact and Recovery One Year after the Hurricanes*, Economics and Statistics Administration, US Department of Commerce, October 2006, accessed August 2, 2016, http://www.esa.doc.gov/sites/default/files/oct2006.pdf.

4. Linda Luther, *Disaster Debris Removal after Hurricane Katrina: Status and Associated Issues*, Congressional Research Service, order code RL33477, updated April 2, 2008, accessed August 2, 2008, https://www.fas.org/sgp/crs/misc/RL33477.pdf.

5. Joseph Lstiburek, "Rebuilding Houston," Building Science Corporation, BSI-101, November 2017.

Miami Beach, FL

Population 91,917

3.937' ABOVE SEA LEVEL

Miami Beach Rising Above

Bruce A. Mowry

In 2013, the city of Miami Beach was doing very little to address sea-level rise and flooding, except talking about the problem with many similar cities in Florida. Through a change requested by residents and elected officials, the city has become a leader in implementing a program to mitigate the water in the streets. It is sometimes said that Miami Beach is a center of applied research to implement solutions for the future. The city is a model to others around the world to show how to "get it done.

Like many South Florida coastal communities, the city of Miami Beach is experiencing the rise in sea level at a rate greater than the global average. The beach, as one of the principal tourist attractions, is the primary driver of the city's economy. The fight is already underway to keep tourists, businesses, and residents dry on sunny days (referred to in Miami Beach as "Sunny Day Flooding"), let alone during storms. Higher tides, prolonged flooding after storms, and beach erosion are among the major effects being experienced. In addition, the porous limestone geology of this low-lying area makes it exceptionally vulnerable to saltwater intrusion into infrastructure systems, surface flooding from rising groundwater, and vegetation loss because of saltwater in root zones.

As a member of the Southeast Florida Regional Climate Change Compact, the city is teaming with other communities to develop a regional governance approach that coordinates mitigation and adaptation activities between Broward, Miami-Dade, Monroe, and Palm Beach Counties. The compact has served to unite, organize, and assess the needs of the region through the lens of climate change and setting the stage for action. In addition to this collaboration, Miami-Dade County intensified efforts to respond to sea-level rise in July 2013 with the formation of the Miami-Dade County Sea Level Rise Task Force. The task force is charged with providing a realistic assessment of the likely impacts of sea-level rise and storm surge over time and making recommendations relative to the comprehensive development master plan, capital facilities planning, and other priorities.

In July 2014, the task force made six recommendations to lay the foundation for action in addressing flood risk, the reinsurance industry, and potential economic implications. In 2016, the city commission formally adopted the sea-level rise projects published by the compact of the counties. By that point, Miami Beach had already started implementing many plan recommendations by modifying city design and construction standards to address sea-level rise.

The city's stormwater management master plan accounted for sea level rise but was inadequate to account for the level of rise that could be expected through the life span of the city's infrastructure. With the backing of the mayor and the city commission, city staffs were encouraged to develop design standards that would account for the forecasted sea-level rise during the next 30 to 50 years, which corresponds to the estimated life span of the utility infrastructure. The stormwater management master plan adopted by the city of Miami Beach in 2010 projected higher groundwater, higher tides, increased flooding, and decreased effectiveness of the existing stormwater system as the results of sea-level rise.

The mayor also formed a Blue-Ribbon Panel on Flooding Mitigation and Sea Level Rise to advise the city in implementing a management plan to address sea-level rise. The panel works with a major consulting firm retained by the city to assist in this planning. Changes to the standards that have already been adopted include the following:

- Stricter design requirements concerning storm rainfall events. The new building code is based on 7.5 inches of rain in a 24-hour period, increased from 6.0 inches.
- Stricter design criteria for tailwater elevation, increased from 0.67 feet to 2.7 feet NAVD88. (Note: NAVD88 refers to the North American Vertical Datum of 1988. It is a datum, or vertical reference line, above which water levels are measured. All further references to NAVD bear the same meaning.)
- An increase in the minimum seawall elevation from 3.5 to 5.7 feet NAVD.
- A new minimum stormwater inlet elevation of 2.7 feet NAVD.

- An increase in the minimum roadway crown elevation from 1.7 feet to 3.7 feet NAVD.
- Improvements to drainage through the installation of pump stations in areas of the city with the highest susceptibility to flooding.

Initial projects have focused on eliminating flooding caused by reverse flows in gravity stormwater outfalls through the implementation of a pumped drainage system. This backflow in outfalls was eliminated by the installation of check valves in the pipes. The city will be looking at addressing private seawalls that are overtopped during high tides and adopting new building standards to prepare for the future. The city has already implemented a program to construct public seawalls to a new minimum elevation 2.5 feet higher than the previous standard. The estimated cost to implement a comprehensive pumped drainage system has been projected at $500 million. The total cost to prepare for higher sea levels by building seawalls to more stringent criteria, raising streets and sidewalks in low areas to higher elevations, setting new building standards to new finished floor elevations, and continuing to address rising groundwater levels directly related to sea-level rise will far exceed the project cost.

Projects incorporating stormwater system improvements and roadway and sidewalk elevation increases are also currently underway. Much of the work is being accomplished using Design-Build project delivery to complete the improvements as quickly as possible. Time is of the essence in keeping ahead of sea-level rise in Miami Beach to ensure that the city's economy is not impacted by the perception that it will not survive a future of flooding, especially from rising groundwater. The response of Miami Beach to rising sea levels focuses on implementing proven approaches, while continuing to look forward at how to best prepare for the effects of future flooding from climate change.

Management of vertical flooding from rising groundwater remains one of the city's greatest challenges. The city is actively monitoring steps taken by other communities, as well as advancements in design technologies. A comprehensive groundwater investigation has been initiated by city staff in coordination with outside experts. This work includes installing wells with monitoring equipment throughout the city to gain information on the underlying hydrogeology and to provide sufficient hydrologic information for conceptualization and calibration of the 3-D density-dependent groundwater flow model being developed by the city. These tools will allow the city to assess the effect of rising groundwater and mitigation strategies that will be implemented.

The efforts are citywide, but one good example is a project taking place in a small neighborhood by the name of Sunset Harbour. Of all the streets in the city that would flood during high tides through the year because of higher sea levels, Sunset Harbour's streets have the lowest elevations. It would be great if this were the only low-elevation neighborhood, but we have others that are close to this same elevation and are suffering from significant flooding. The neighborhood is close to the bay and has many kayak rental businesses. During high tides, some people take their kayaks and paddle down some of the streets. The neighborhood said that enough was enough and came together to support a major reconstruction and raising of the streets and the addition of stormwater pumping systems. A typical cross section of one of the streets is shown in figure 6.1. Now, visitors from around the world come to Sunset Harbour to see what can be done with an effective plan of action.

After the city installed a new drainage system with pumps and raised the first street, a petition with over a thousand signatures was delivered immediately to the mayor and commissioners requesting that they reconstruct the entire neighborhood following the model of the work just completed. Contrary to the common situation in many communities, the

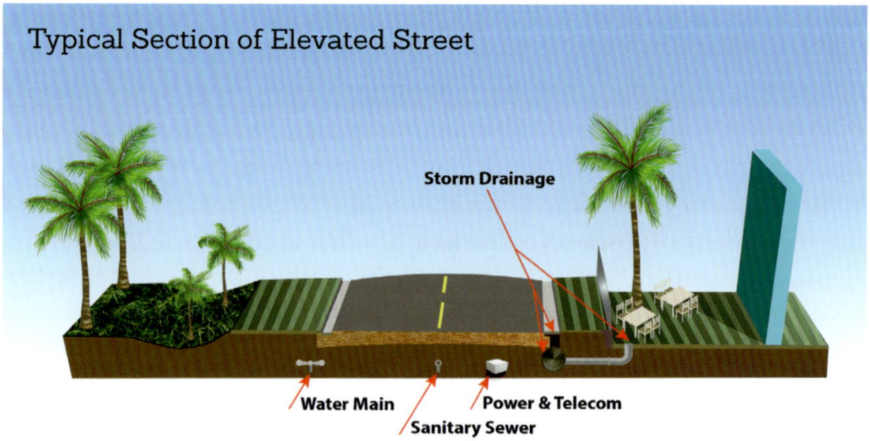

Figure 6.1. Sketch of a typical cross section of a street showing underground utilities that must be upgraded, and split sidewalks to accommodate the lower existing building elevations.

residents and businesses *wanted* the construction in their neighborhood.

When guests come to look at the neighborhood, they are told that this is a five-step program. As they are escorted over to a set of five stairs from the existing elevation of the older buildings to the new elevated sidewalk with the street, they can count the five steps. The actual program is as follows:

1. Improve drainage with new, larger pipes under the streets and new pump stations.
2. Install check valves in all the gravity outfalls to stop backflow during high tides.
3. Raise the streets up to 30 inches higher to meet the city's new minimum street criteria.
4. Install steps and ADA ramps on sidewalks to allow easy access from the old lower elevation to the new higher elevation.
5. Install landscaping and lights at higher elevations out of the rising salty groundwater resulting from sea-level rise.

To be truthful, the real first step is to meet with the residents and businesses in multiple public meetings to discuss our actions and get their input and support on the neighborhood changes. If the support of the residents is not established at the beginning, it is difficult to have a successful project. City staff walks the neighborhood during the project to get input from the residents, businesses, and visitors, and adjustments are made if necessary. If you ensure the support of the neighborhood, the support of the politicians is easy.

In the city of Miami Beach, success is measured by results in mitigating the challenges of sea-level rise in a city that is constructed on porous limestone only a few feet above mean sea level. The important note is that if you design to meet mean sea level, the results will be a city that floods twice a day during high tide. An idea often expressed in Miami Beach is "Great things will happen when you work outside your comfort zone." Miami Beach is working outside its comfort zone to achieve the great things necessary to ensure the survival of a great city.

Figure 6.2. Reconstruction of streets and sidewalks as they are raised to the new, higher elevations.

Editor's Note

In early 2018, Miami Beach's project to elevate streets, revamp stormwater drainage systems, and build a new seawall slowed amid concerns about inadequate permitting for the work. The city is working to correct the problems, including the relocation of the seawall sections. To review the project and guide its next steps, the city secured a grant through the Rockefeller Foundation's 100 Resilient Cities initiative to organize a review panel featuring experts from the Urban Land Institute.

Houston, TX

MSA Population 6,928,233

80' ABOVE SEA LEVEL

Hurricane Harvey

Arts and Cultural Recovery Six Months after the Storm

Debbie McNulty

Harvey Arrives

Hurricane Harvey is the most extreme rain event in US history. The storm made landfall the night of Friday, August 25, 2017, near Rockport, Texas, as a category 4 storm with crippling winds of 130 mph that damaged 80 percent of Aransas County. On Saturday, the storm was downgraded to a tropical storm and stalled over Houston for four days. Dire rainfall predictions turned into reality and the protracted storm delivered

Figure 7.1. Flooding from Hurricane Harvey devastated Houston-area neighborhoods. (Dominick Del Vecchio/FEMA)

unprecedented devastation, overwhelming communities well accustomed to substantial flood events.

A recap of the storm prepared by the Weather Channel details the event. It dropped 40 to 61 inches of rain in southeast Texas and southwest Louisiana and then triggered flash flooding in parts of Arkansas, Kentucky, and Tennessee on August 31 and September 1. In total, it broke all-time US tropical cyclone rain records.[1] Federal and local agencies in Texas estimated that more than 13,000 people were rescued from floodwaters. The *Houston Chronicle* reported that approximately 75 people died as a result of the storm and that most of the 50 victims in the Houston area had drowned.[2] On January 17, 2018, Texas governor Greg Abbott extended the state disaster declaration for Texas counties affected by Hurricane Harvey. Texas counties declared disaster areas are eligible for assistance as they recover and rebuild after a storm. There were 60 counties included in the state disaster declaration.[3]

Figure 7.2. US soldiers assigned to the Texas Army National Guard arrived in Houston to aid citizens in areas heavily flooded by Hurricane Harvey on August 27, 2017. (US Army National Guard photo by 1st Lt. Zachary West, www.dvidshub.net)

Figure 7.3. Hurricane Harvey made landfall on August 31, 2017 and caused unprecedented flooding in Houston, as seen here in an aerial photograph on the outskirts of the city. (US Army National Guard photo courtesy of SC-HART)

Hurricane Harvey is also the largest housing disaster in American history. In Houston alone, the storm damaged 345,000 housing units, destroyed more than a million cars, and caused $2.5 billion in damage. Harris County Flood Control District estimates that one trillion gallons of water were dumped on that county alone in four days—an amount that would cover Harris County's 1,800 square miles with an average of 33 inches of water. More homes flooded in Houston during Hurricane Harvey than in New Orleans during Hurricane Katrina or in New York City during Superstorm Sandy.

Six months after the storm, Houston mayor Sylvester Turner reported on recovery efforts, including the city's collection of its entire $100 million insurance policy, the submission of 8,897 Harvey-related permitting applications, the opening of 12 neighborhood recovery centers, and the launch of a new volunteer campaign called Houston Still Needs You to pair volunteers with relief agencies. City officials are hoping that volunteer hours can substitute for dollars in the 10 percent share the city pays on projects involving federal disaster grants. Because of the immense damage cost, the 10 percent share will equal the staggering figure of $200–300 million. The joint city-county Hurricane Harvey Relief Fund raised $112 million from 125,000 donors and is preparing a fourth round of grants. With thousands of individuals living in homes in need of repairs and 3,422 families still living in hotels, frustration with the slow pace of federal funds is only increasing.

On the policy side, local and state leaders seem less inclined to continue averting their eyes from decades-long practices that contributed to the extraordinary damage toll of Hurricane Harvey. For Houston, the storm was the third—and by far the most costly and wide-reaching—flood event in three consecutive years. Resident engagement in developing solutions has never been higher and citizens are putting serious interventions on the table, including the regulation of development, massive buyouts of flood-prone properties, and following through on previously identified flood-prevention projects that have never been built. Harris County's pending bond election and corresponding tax increase will be the first test of whether voters are willing to invest in the costly measures required to interrupt what has become an annual trend.

The Hurricane's Impact on Arts and Culture

Within this context of storm recovery, the region's cultural community —its artists, historic preservationists, culture bearers, and presenting organizations—have resumed services while simultaneously repairing structures, rebuilding revenue streams, and taking stock of what a five- to ten-year recovery projection means for their economic future and morale reserves.

When Hurricane Harvey dropped historic amounts of rainfall on the greater Houston area, hundreds of artists and nonprofit arts and culture organizations suffered extensive damage and disruption. The recovery process will be difficult, costly, and, for many, slow. Many artists are underinsured, and FEMA disaster assistance will not cover losses such as studio repairs, equipment, materials, or loss of earned revenue. Moreover, the steep drop in earned revenue poses a crisis for small and midsize arts organizations, and few have sufficient savings or cash reserves to sustain them during a long disruption. Also, either they are not likely to qualify for insurance products such as business interruption coverage, or the policies they can get are not cost-effective. This disruption in the nonprofit sector has ripple effects too—for artists, since many are self-employed and support themselves with contract work, as well as for staff and local businesses.

Data collected on the nonprofit cultural sector by the Mayor's Office of Cultural Affairs and the Harvey Arts Recovery Fund found 71 primarily Harris County–based organizations reporting storm impact for preparation, cleanup, damage, and service interruption of more than $56 million. These early estimates have only increased, and the immense challenge of resuming operations in order to generate cash flow has strained the sector significantly.

Eight large organizations, mostly in the Houston Theater District, account for more than $45 million of the impact reported: Alley Theatre, Houston Ballet, Houston Grand Opera, Houston Symphony, Museum of Fine Arts Houston, Children's Museum, Hobby Center for the Performing Arts, and Theatre Under the Stars. Of the more than $10 million of storm impact to small and midsize groups, nearly 40 percent is attributed to service interruption experienced by 63 groups.

Among the hardest-hit organizations was Alley Theatre, which was able to hold its season-opening production at the University of Houston in September and to reopen its upstairs Hubbard Theatre in November and its downstairs Neuhaus Stage in January. The Wortham Theater Center, home to the Houston Ballet and Houston Grand Opera, which sustained substantial damage after taking on 12 feet of water, is undergoing major repairs and is expected to remain closed until September 2018. The Houston Ballet and Houston Grand Opera scrambled to find temporary homes at other venues, and the opera constructed the HGO Resilience Theater at the George R. Brown Convention Center by transforming an exhibit hall into a 1,700-seat theater.

Harvey Arts Recovery Fund Is Born

Worried about the hurricane's impact on the arts and culture ecosystem of the Houston region, and particularly its artists and small and midsize nonprofit organizations, a group of partners came together to launch the Harvey Arts Recovery Fund (HARF). This collaborative effort is led by the Center for Art and Social Engagement at the University of Houston,

CultureWorks Greater Houston, Dance Source Houston, Fresh Arts, Galveston Historical Foundation, Houston Arts Alliance, and the Houston Mayor's Office of Cultural Affairs. Houston Arts Alliance (HAA) is the fund's fiscal administrator.

HARF is a unique peer-based, locally rooted, multidisciplinary partnership providing crucial resources to help artists, and the arts organizations that employ so many of them, recover from the hurricane and get back to work. The fund provides grants to help cover rebuilding and recovery costs that are not covered by FEMA or private insurance so that artists can get back to work. Artists and smaller arts organizations in a 10-county area (Harris, Fort Bend, Montgomery, Brazoria, Galveston, Liberty, Waller, Chambers, Austin, and San Jacinto Counties) are eligible for support. In January 2018, HARF awarded more than $40,000 to local artists and arts, heritage, and cultural organizations that suffered personal and professional losses from Hurricane Harvey, and in February a second application period was opened.

Organizations included in the first round of grants were Art League Houston, Dance Houston, Houston Maritime Museum, Cypress Creek FACE, Pearl Fincher Museum of Fine Arts, Dickinson Historical Society, Dream Studio, Houston Aeronautical Heritage Society, Evelyn Rubenstein Jewish Community Center of Houston, FrenetiCore, Heritage Society, and Mystic Lyon. HARF received 65 applications for individual grants. The list of recipients included photographers, musicians, and public art installers. Requests were for studio repairs, replacement of equipment, materials and musical instruments, and digitization of artwork.

HARVEY ARTS RECOVERY

arts culture food
CHOOSE LOCAL
Put your $ where your ♥ is.

HARF actions were instrumental in bringing new preservation grants to Houston cultural institutions. The John Biggers mural at the Blue Triangle Community Center in Third Ward, long imperiled by the lack of funds to fix a leaky roof and now peppered with mold, prompted the National Endowment for the Humanities (NEH) to announce in February 2018 a new infrastructure grant program to support building upgrades at the nation's cultural institutions. "Absolutely, the Biggers mural played a decisive role in creating this new category at the agency," said Jon Parrish Peede, who leads the NEH. "It's such an uncommon work for its time." Biggers is considered one of the foremost artists to capture the black experience of the twentieth century.

Beyond financial assistance, HARF is addressing artists' longer-term employment needs by connecting them with resources and looking to foster better disaster preparedness and coordination in the cultural sector and with local and national disaster response agencies. HARF developed a Choose Local logo so the city and region could launch a campaign to support local arts, culture, and food businesses. The infrastructure created through this collaboration will make the region's arts ecosystem stronger and more resilient, and thus better equipped for future disasters. Further, it will provide a model for other communities across the country.

Notes

1. "Historic Hurricane Harvey's Recap," Weather Channel, September 2, 2017, accessed March 8, 2018, https://weather.com/storms/hurricane/news/tropical-storm-harvey-forecast-texas-louisiana-arkansas.

2. Cindy George, Margaret Kadifa, Lindsay Ellis, and Keri Blakinger, "Storm Deaths: Harvey Claims Lives of More Than 75 in Texas," *Houston Chronicle*, updated October 9, 2017, accessed March 8, 2018, https://www.chron.com/news/houston-weather/hurricaneharvey/article/Harvey-Aftermath-Houston-police-officer-dies-19–12159139.php.

3. Angelina, Aransas, Atascosa, Austin, Bastrop, Bee, Bexar, Brazoria, Brazos, Burleson, Caldwell, Calhoun, Cameron, Chambers, Colorado, Comal, DeWitt, Fayette, Fort Bend, Galveston, Goliad, Gonzales, Grimes, Guadalupe, Hardin, Harris, Jackson, Jasper, Jefferson, Jim Wells, Karnes, Kerr, Kleberg, Lavaca, Lee, Leon, Liberty, Live Oak, Madison, Matagorda, Milam, Montgomery, Newton, Nueces, Orange, Polk, Refugio, Sabine, San Augustine, San Jacinto, San Patricio, Trinity, Tyler, Victoria, Walker, Waller, Washington, Wharton, Willacy, and Wilson Counties.

Netherlands

Population 17.02 million

-19.685' BELOW SEA LEVEL (lowest point)

The Dutch Tradition of Flood Control

Shifting Attitudes toward Flood Risk Reduction

B. L. M. "Bee" Kothuis
and A. D. "Nikki" Brand

Introduction

This contribution aims to give a better understanding of the Dutch tradition of flood protection and to provide inspiration for communities challenged by living in a flood-prone environment. The Netherlands, a small but densely populated country in northwest Europe, provides a road map toward successful reduction of flood risk. The country is within the Rhine-Meuse delta, a dangerous but advantageous site where the water provides opportunities but introduces risk. The nation contains about 17 million people in an area roughly the size of four to six Texas counties.

The Dutch must protect against flooding on a wide scale, as over half of the national territory lies below sea level or is flood prone. As such, the people of the Netherlands have fought flood risk for centuries and in the process have acquired an international reputation in the field of flood risk reduction.

It may thus appear that the "Dutch tradition" is fairly straightforward, established and more or less invariable over time. However, the Netherlands has not taken just one approach to mitigation, as perspectives have shifted continually over the centuries. In fact, history provides a rich set of examples of how the Dutch have dealt with flood risk, and the various consequences of those differing approaches.

This chapter combines insights derived from practices of historical geography and anthropology and builds on the knowledge of a greater research project toward flood risk reduction in the greater Houston–Galveston Bay region.[1] We will start by introducing how the Dutch tradition of flood protection changed in three stages, based on insights from the study of the spatial impact of that tradition. Second, we will explain in greater detail how the Dutch attitude regarding "dry feet" has evolved since the 1950s, based on insights from the study of discourses in public debate. Finally, we will conclude with lessons that can be learned from these insights and discuss how they can be applied elsewhere.

Strikingly, once the map of the Houston–Galveston Bay region is turned upside down, one can see that it shares many geographical similarities with the Netherlands (fig. 8.1). Both are fairly urbanized regions surrounding a central body of water, with barrier islands bordering on the ocean or a large gulf. Both contain heavily populated flood-prone areas that must deal with sea-level rise and increased storm activity, but at the same time they are places of increasing economic, social, and environmental value. Both the Netherlands and the Houston–Galveston Bay region have a need for flood risk reduction while retaining navigational access for large ports with important industrial activities. Both areas contain a rich natural environment, providing wetlands and salt marshes as crucial habitats in delicate ecosystems. Finally, both are regions hit by catastrophic storm surges: the Netherlands was last struck in 1953 and the Galveston Bay region by Hurricane Ike in 2008.

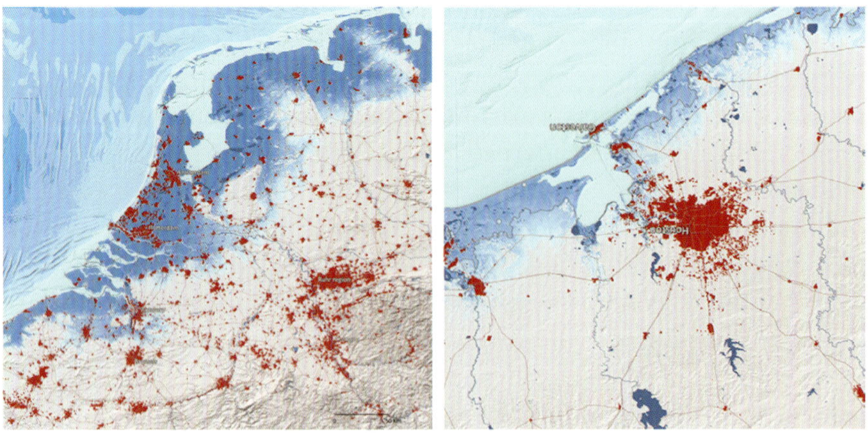

Figure 8.1. Map of the Netherlands (left) and upside-down map of the Houston–Galveston Bay region (right). (Courtesy of S. Nijenhuis and M. Pouderoijen, TU Delft)

However, these regions also have differences, of which two seem to be key. First, in the Netherlands, flood events are considered failures of the system, not acts of nature or of God. Second, what took the Netherlands centuries to develop, the Houston–Galveston Bay region may have to do in years.

Changing Dutch Traditions of Flood Protection

Most people will be surprised to learn that since the 1990s, Dutch coastal flood defense has not necessarily resembled the "hard" constructions of the Delta Works (fig. 8.2). Rather, a Dutch coastal waterfront typically resembles a so-called hybrid flood defense, as in the dike-in-dune constructions in the seaside resorts of Noordwijk and Katwijk (fig. 8.3) or the dike-in-boulevard of Scheveningen (fig. 8.4).

Often when the Dutch tradition of flood protection is discussed, the image of the Eastern Scheldt environmental barrier comes to mind (fig. 8.5). This half-open storm surge gate is part of the Delta Works, a series of 14 sluices, dams, and storm surge gates built primarily of concrete and basalt

Figure 8.2. The Delta Works: Eastern Scheldt Barrier, concrete pillars. (Courtesy B. L. M. Kothuis)

Figure 8.3. Katwijk dike-in-dune construction phase. (Courtesy Beeldbank Rijkswaterstaat)

Figure 8.4. Dike-in-boulevard in the coastal city of Scheveningen. (Courtesy B. L. M. Kothuis)

Figure 8.5. Aerial view of the Eastern Scheldt barrier. (Courtesy Beeldbank Rijkswaterstaat)

blocks after the flood disaster of 1953. The barrier shortened the coastline by approximately 435 miles and has been put forward as a UNESCO World Heritage Site.

Recent spatial interventions on behalf of flood control are more diverse but share several properties: (1) they aim to fulfill multiple purposes in one intervention; (2) they are designed with respect for the natural environment; (3) they merge with their spatial surroundings or allow more space for the water.

More recent Dutch coastal waterfronts typically resemble a hybrid flood defense. For example, the flood defense in the seaside resort of Scheveningen is a 1.5-mile dike-in-boulevard construction, complemented with nine billion cubic feet of beach nourishment. It aims to improve public space and boost business. Another example is the dike-in-dune defense in Katwijk. It also aims to fulfill several purposes in one intervention, as it houses a garage, thereby removing parked vehicles from the surface above, and thus creates an improved public space. A third example is the Sand Engine (fig. 8.6), a mega sand nourishment project that strategically places an extremely large amount of sand in a precise location that optimizes the movement of water currents to redistribute it over the next two to three decades.

Figure 8.6. Sand Engine. (Courtesy Beeldbank Rijkswaterstaat)

This innovation—the diversification and increased multifunctionality of flood control measures after the 1990s—was in fact a revolutionary response to the Dutch tradition that had been followed since the 1890s. It represents a third phase in a centuries-old tradition. Over the vast majority of the decades from 1800 until today, flood control in the Netherlands has been planned, financed, executed, and maintained in a highly centralized manner. As a result, the number of floods and the impacts of those floods have diminished substantially. However, this also explains why flood defenses erected or updated in the twentieth century appear to be less uniform and standardized, and why initiatives for spatial interventions on behalf of flood control meet with public concern.

Three Phases of Spatial Change

In the first phase that we consider here, prior to the 1890s, the Dutch tradition of flood protection was systematic yet primarily regionally focused. As early as the fourteenth century, landowners and other stakeholders joined forces to erect levees and dikes, followed by the construction of windmills to pump out excess water in the 1500s. Such polders—units of land surrounded by flood defenses—were maintained by public organizations called Water Boards (not unlike the Levee Improvement Districts, or LIDs, in places such as Fort Bend County, Texas). These Water Boards—a form of special-purpose government—developed in the Netherlands simultaneously with, yet independently from, general-purpose governments such as municipalities and counties. By the sixteenth century, this had caused the low-lying parts of the Netherlands to geographically resemble a sheet of "bubble wrap," as separate polders clustered into a seemingly coherent whole.

Settlements developed primarily inland, and trade and industry flourished. Flood protection measures such as dams required transshipment of goods, as such locations were often break-in-bulk sites where methods of transportation had to change. The coastal zone itself was generally avoided. True waterfront towns and cities emerged only where the opportunity for fast economic profit compensated for the risk of flooding. Often the entire waterfront was raised using landfill. Elsewhere an earthen dike with a protective row of poles was the norm.

This regional distribution of responsibilities was based on strong local government, and the system was moderately successful until the second half of the eighteenth century. Small flood events occurred but people dealt with them. They created a so-called *amphibious culture*. By the end of the eighteenth century, economic stagnation, civil war, and the shipworm had undermined the maintenance of flood defenses, and several large flood events were reported.

After the 1800s, the Dutch tradition of flood protection changed character because of the foundation of the Rijkswaterstaat, the National Corps of Engineers, in 1798. In this second phase, it became centralized and standardized. The attitude turned from offensive—trying to save what is ours—to manipulative. Spatial interventions were no longer confined to those spots where flood control was needed most. Instead, the entire water system was altered and modified to meet required protection standards demanded by national law.

This period is known mostly for its achievements in mega engineering, such as the Southern Sea (Zuiderzee) Works (1920s–1960s) and the Delta Works (1950s–1997). The Southern Sea Works generated the Closure Dam (fig. 8.7), a flood defense 19 miles long and 24 feet high that turned a rebellious inland sea into a huge freshwater reservoir. The Delta Works comprises 14 large dams, sluices, and storm surge barriers. The Brouwersdam, for example, is so big that it is used for music festivals

Figure 8.7. Closure Dam (Afsluitdijk) with locks at Kornwerderzand. (Courtesy Beeldbank Rijkswaterstaat)

during summer. Both of these grand works shortened the coastline substantially and thus diminished the total length of flood defense that was to be maintained according to the highest safety standards. In the second half of the twentieth century, all flood defenses that were considered primary to the nation's safety were heightened to *delta height*, the minimum safe height, which is at least 38 feet (11.5 meters). The concrete and basalt flood defense at the naval town of Den Helder, for example, is 39 feet high (fig. 8.8). And at almost 40 feet high and 3.1 miles long, the Westkapelle Sea Dike along the North Sea literally dwarfs the town of Westkapelle (fig. 8.9). Such primary flood defenses at delta height were not only standardized but were also explicitly made to be single purpose, higher, broader, and surrounded by land-use restrictions.

Changes in the Dutch tradition of flood protection between 1800 and 1990 from regionally focused and locally adapted to centralized and standardized, and from offensive to manipulative, were driven by increased urgency and centralization. This required and brought about considerable innovations. The Dutch economy expanded once more, as did the built-up area. Existing settlements became cities, but also, for the first

Figure 8.8. Helderse Sea Dike at Den Helder, 39 feet high. (Courtesy Beeldbank Rijkswaterstaat)

Figure 8.9. Westkapelle Sea Dike at Westkapelle, Zeeland, 3.1 miles long and almost 40 feet high. (Courtesy Beeldbank Rijkswaterstaat)

Figure 8.10. Kurhaus on the beach in Scheveningen. (Courtesy Beeldbank Rijkswaterstaat)

time in centuries, the lure of living near the sea drove settlements into flood-prone areas that in earlier times were considered too dangerous for permanent use. A famous example is Scheveningen, the seaside resort with its prominent Kurhaus right at the beachfront (fig. 8.10). Also, as inland areas accumulated more value, flood events caused more damage, and the urgency for comprehensive action substantially increased.

Geographic upscaling of water management came with the rise of the Dutch national state. Eager to prove its legitimacy, the new state erected the Rijkswaterstaat, the National Corps of Engineers that was to address water management issues. This was a task of utmost national importance according to the new constitution, as it came just after defending the nation against foreign enemies. Before the Second World War and the German occupation, the corps had already achieved considerable feats. It had altered the distribution of tidal inlets in the delta, boosting Rotterdam's role as the national harbor. Inland lakes were impoldered and a grand boulevard was built in The Hague. Large-scale land reclamation and flood protection systems were implemented, such as the Haarlemmermeer, where the international airport Schiphol was placed. But the National Corps' biggest and most heroic achievement in the first part of the twentieth century was no doubt the restraining of the rebellious inland Southern Sea into a freshwater reservoir. This endeavor, named the Southern Sea Works, had extensive spatial impact; in the process of reducing flood risk the corps acquired an enormous area of "new land." In fact, a 12th province, consisting of two large polders, was added to the national territory.

Although the foundations for the new Dutch tradition of coastal flood control in its second phase were laid before the 1950s, the trauma of the 1953 flood event was the catalyst that legitimized spatial intervention on behalf of flood control on an unprecedented scale. This was the moment that such intervention reached its zenith, and its spatial impact increased and intensified. Before we elaborate on this process, we need to sketch an image of one of the most impressive natural events in recent Dutch history in order to understand the context, the sociocultural setting of the time in which it took place, and the response it evoked.

The 1953 Flood Disaster and the Delta Works

In the 1950s, the Dutch were seen, and saw themselves, as the best and most innovative hydraulic engineers in the world. The shortening of the northern coastline by the so-called Closure Dam in the northern Netherlands was an international engineering phenomenon at the time. There had been no more land loss, but substantial landmass was reclaimed and new settlements arose in the lowest polders, in the dunes, and behind the flood defenses.

Then came the 1953 disaster. With more than 1,800 deaths and over 100,000 people displaced, Dutch national pride and identity were severely harmed. It was a strong blow for a country that was just scrambling to its feet right after the devastating and humiliating Second World War. And there was economic harm. Of course, the Dutch lost many buildings and a large amount of land and infrastructure, but there was more. Major damage to one of the Netherlands' main export products was expected, as this event threatened to reduce the credibility of Dutch hydraulic engineers. Who would trust them for expertise on dredging, reclaiming land, and building dikes, dams, and harbors all over the world if they could not even protect their own country? A grand reply was needed.

That grand reply had already been designed but was shelved as a result of the Second World War and the lack of internal support. The 1953 disaster turned out to be its "window of opportunity." The so-called Delta Plan was a second immense shortening of the Dutch coastline by grand and innovative waterworks, this time in the southwestern Netherlands, where the disaster had struck.

However, a lot of money was needed to make this work: three billion guilders was estimated at the time, equivalent to US$13.2 billion in 2018. This was a lot of money just after the Second World War, when all supplies were focused on and needed for postwar reconstruction. To convince the public (as well as politicians and, probably unwittingly, themselves) that this money was well spent, Dutch government officials repeatedly and explicitly promised one thing: with the Delta Works implemented, the Netherlands would be safe.

Although the implementation of the plan was expected to take about 25 years, it took about 45. And all this time, for almost half a century, the lifetime of at least three generations, this same message—"Delta Works means you are safe"—was repeated, over and over again. Just as American cities mark specific historic disasters as cultural and emotional reference points—for example, Galveston's 1900 Hurricane—the 1953 Flood Disaster was a pivotal event in the history of the Netherlands. In fact, the response to this disaster has been decisive in attitudes toward flood safety ever since.

Three Discourses: Fight, Victory, and Threat

To create a new perspective on the shifting attitude in the Dutch flood safety doctrine, we explain the three dominant discourses on flood safety in the Netherlands since the 1950s, starting with the discourse of "fight," followed by that of "victory" in the 1970s and 1980s, and ending with the most contemporary one, the discourse of "threat" (fig. 8.11).

The discourse of fight was the dominant discourse from the 1950s to the end of the 1960s—a time when Dutch society was strongly paternalistic, trust in engineers and experts was immense, and rational, technological, or so-called hard solutions were seen as the best way to cope with flood risk. This perspective prevailed, as the memory of water as a threatening natural phenomenon was close. Water was "the enemy." People would even speak of the "Water Wolf." It is quite comprehensible that from this perspective, a grand project such as the Delta Works sprouted.

The Dutch flood safety debate

Research-categories / **Dominant discourses**	1953 – end of the 60's **Discourse of fight**	Begin 70's – begin 90's **Discourse of victory**	Mid 90's – >> **Discourse of threat**
Environment	Fighting nature *Water is enemy*	Protecting nature *Water is friend*	Cooperating with nature *Water is 'dangerous' ally*
Controllability	Rational ideal of control	Romantic ideal of control	Flexibility as ideal of control
Accountability	Supremacy *of God and nature*	Professionals responsible: *Government & Engineers*	Shared responsibility: *Professionals and Citizens*

Dutch spatial interventions

On behalf of Coastal Flood Defense	Standardized, Uniform		Diversified, Multifunctional

Figure 8.11. An overview of the three main discourses in the Netherlands since 1953 (fight, victory, and threat), and the patterns of meaning given to topics in three key research categories. To decipher these discourses, a thorough examination of the Dutch public and experts' debates on flood risk was performed, focusing on patterns in what they appeared to take for granted with their underlying assumptions, and how these were expressed in technologies, policies, and flood risk management. Added in blue are the last two phases of spatial change brought about in the Netherlands by spatial intervention on behalf of flood risk reduction. Not surprisingly, these run parallel.

However, at the beginning of the 1970s a new discourse started to become dominant—the discourse of victory. Since the Dutch engineers had done their job so well, there had been no flooding for many years. The continual message "by installing the Delta Works we are safe" had been conveyed, and it had sunk in. So, the general feeling in Dutch society was a flush of victory "we have won from the water." One of the reports of the Dutch National Corps of Engineers even stated, "The Netherlands is completed," and the quite presumptuous saying "God created the world, but the Dutch created the Netherlands" was making the rounds. Government and experts took all responsibility for flood safety, implying that citizens could "leave it to us and sleep sound behind the levee."

This was also the time the emancipation movement came up in all different shapes and forms. People tried to liberate themselves from all kinds of ties and also wanted to liberate nature. And where before vulnerable humans had to be protected against dangerous nature, it was now felt that vulnerable nature had to be protected against destructive humans. As their perspective changed, people favored "soft, romantic, and green" measures over the previous "hard, rational, and technological" measures to deal with nature. This shift in viewpoint gave space for the so-called landscape, nature, and culture values to be taken into account. The public felt that some levees could even be lowered, for the sake of historical value. And in the 1970s it was decided that the Eastern Scheldt, as part of the protective structure of the Delta Works, should not just keep water out as a protective measure, since that would harm the natural environment of the bay behind. A whole new construction had to be designed, which led to an environmental barrier, with gates that could be opened and closed to allow the tide to enter in a regulated way. That really added to the cost. The final cost for the Delta Works is now estimated at about $43 billion, three times as much as originally planned, and about 75 percent of that was spent for the Eastern Scheldt environmental barrier.

Then, two major near disasters occurred along the Rhine and Meuse Rivers in 1993 and 1995. Approximately 250,000 people were evacuated, as the river water rose nearly to the top of the levees. In the aftermath, people felt they had "dodged the bullet." Although there was a short revival of the discourse of fight, most citizens quickly got back to their convenient feeling of victory. And officials and experts would only affirm this, continually saying that the levees had done their job in the end and that the Netherlands was still the best protected and safest country in the world. However, within the ranks of experts, many people realized that things could have been much worse.

These near disasters turned out to be the first of several drivers of change around the turn of the century. Other major drivers included the disastrous tsunami in Southeast Asia in 2004 and, of course, Hurricane Katrina in New Orleans in 2005. Katrina reinforced the message that extreme flood disasters could happen in the Western world. Finally, more attention was given to the climate change debate, as American ex–vice president Al Gore traveled the world with his message of fear.

Among Dutch policy makers and flood risk experts, a discourse of threat developed as they asked, "What if this happened in the Netherlands?" Yet it is not easy for flood risk experts in the Netherlands to convey the message that a life-threatening flood could be possible. It is a dilemma. On the one hand, government and experts do not want to admit that a flood disaster could happen, since that would mean they did not live up to their promises and tasks. On the other hand, they need to admit that even in the very well flood-protected Netherlands, a flood disaster is possible, since the consequences of such a disaster would be financially disastrous if only the government was held responsible.[2] So they have to involve the public, trying to make people become aware of their own responsibilities for flood safety. In the discourse of threat, responsibilities therefore have to be shared. The message is "we are all in this together."

As for the environment, the assumption is that people and nature have to work together, a perspective found in the phrases "Building with Nature" and "Engineering with Nature." In this regard, nature is viewed as both a friend and an enemy: a dangerous ally. And as for the ability to control flooding, there has been a shift toward flexibility. If prevention is not possible, then the aim becomes to control what comes *after* the flood by means of various spatial planning and evacuation measures.

As such, the discourse of threat has stimulated the rise of diversified spatial interventions on behalf of flood risk reduction. In this view, simply building and maintaining a dike to prevent flooding is no longer enough. The contemporary Dutch tradition of flood control includes natural and nature-based solutions, even allowing the water in at certain sites. Multifunctional projects such as "Room for the River" do not attempt just to keep all water out of a system, but to give the water space to move.

The Perception Gap

As a result of the safety doctrine, a perception gap exists between government and society at the beginning of the twenty-first century. The discourse of threat drives the decision making of most experts and governments. As such, there is much discussion about risks concerning climate change and the need for more shared responsibility. Under this perspective, not only experts must realize what it means to live in a vulnerable delta; society as a whole needs to become aware of these risks. Because of this enhanced flood awareness, it is expected that people and organizations will increasingly develop "risk-aware behavior."

On the other hand, the discourse of victory still dominates the perspective of most citizens. For example, multiple surveys show that the Dutch public does not commonly view flooding as a severe threat. On the contrary, most citizens trust experts and governments blindly when it comes to the management of flood safety issues, rather than think about flood risk and appropriate behavioral adaptations. They put nice wooden floors in their houses and object to cutting dangerous deep-rooted trees on dikes because "it spoils the view." Architects design emergency backup power units in the basements of hospitals in flood-prone areas, and not too long ago, the central government's planning agencies encouraged building projects in the nation's deepest polders. These actions show a perception that the battle is over and the fight has been won. The notion of severe flood threat does not come to mind. Instead, the prevailing view is "We've beaten the water, the experts will solve any problems, and the Netherlands has the best engineers, don't we?"

In the meantime, the discourse of threat strongly affects flood safety strategies chosen by Dutch policy makers and other experts. A range of new concepts for flood risk reduction has emerged under the assumptions belonging to that discourse. *Building with Nature* is one of these concepts, as is the concept of *Multilayer Safety*, which is supposedly the basic and major principle for virtually every current Dutch flood risk policy (fig. 8.12). Multilayer safety aims to be flexible and adaptive, and to embrace the widest range of possible solutions in three layers:

1. Structural and nature-based flood defenses for prevention of a flood;
2. Spatial planning measures for mitigation; and
3. Evacuation strategies to enact when all other measures have failed.

This probably sounds familiar to people in the United States. However, the second and third layers are quite new in the Netherlands and in fact are still in their baby steps. These new concepts provide an opportunity to vigorously invent and improve flood risk reduction measures, often with international cooperation. For example, the Netherlands learns from Texas, where the public is relatively risk aware and experts have developed methods to streamline this behavior for maximum public benefit during a disaster. On the other hand, Texans can learn from the Dutch

Figure 8.12. Multilayer Safety: Layer 1. Flood defense structures; 2. Spatial planning; 3. Evacuation plans. (Courtesy Ministry of Infrastructure and the Environment, Netherlands)

experience, too, particularly the consequences of promoting flood risk reduction measures as a "safety guarantee," which makes citizens become nonresponsive and reckless despite increasing risk because they feel completely safe behind a system of flood barriers.

Conclusion

So how have the Dutch been able to live in such a flood-prone environment for centuries? And what lessons can be learned by the greater Houston–Galveston Bay region and other flood-prone areas of the United States?

To move forward with new plans, we must once again revisit the particular circumstances that make each region different. Focusing on their differences is key in making this application, because if not for these differences, the strategies that worked well in the Netherlands could be immediately applied everywhere else.

As previously stated, two features of the Netherlands seem to be key:

1. Flood events are considered failures of the system, not acts of God or nature, and
2. What the Netherlands took centuries to develop, other areas may have to do in years.

Although people in vulnerable coastal cities may feel pressure to act quickly, they might want to remember that attitudes toward flood risk reduction are not fixed but rather evolve and transform, thus allowing for innovation and change. This evolution is clearly seen in the history of flood protection in the Netherlands. Therefore, it is important to keep in mind that future perspectives may differ from the outlook today.

We hope that communities can draw inspiration from the Netherlands for flood risk reduction but also learn from its mistakes. Ultimately it is up to those who actually live in each place to sense and decide which solutions and designs they should choose. We hope the Dutch tradition will inspire them.

Notes

1. The research has produced the book *Delft Delta Design: Houston Galveston Bay Region, Texas, USA*. This book is an evocative and richly illustrated account of many years of collaboration between Delft University and the Severe Storm Prediction, Education, and Evacuation from Disasters (SSPEED) Center at Rice University in Houston, and Texas A&M University at Galveston (TAMUG). In the aftermath of the hurricane, these two universities led several initiatives to propose and design flood mitigation strategies. In collaboration with TAMUG and the SSPEED Center, students and researchers at Delft University of Technology in the Netherlands have been investigating and designing regional strategies for flood risk reduction. In this publication, they and their Texas counterparts reflect on the research, design, and insight that have sprouted from this collective endeavor. The book consists of three parts: a more technically oriented section, "Hydraulic Infrastructures"; a section oriented more toward support of governance and decision making, "Multifunctional Flood Defenses," and a spatial planning and architecture section, "Delta Interventions Studio." The book is available in pdf form at repository.tudelft.nl or in hard copy at www.bol.com.

2. In the Netherlands, no national flood risk insurance schemes exist. In case of a flood disaster, victims can appeal to a national emergency fund; however, there is no guarantee for compensation of losses.

Bibliography

Bosch, A., and W. van der Ham. *Twee eeuwen Rijkswaterstaat 1798–1998*. Europese Bibliotheek, Zaltbommel, 1998.

Brand, N., ed. *European References: International Workshop on Coastal Quality*. Atelier Kustkwaliteit, Delft, 2012.

Carasso-Kok, M., ed. *Geschiedenis van Amsterdam. Tot 1578. Een stad uit het niets*. Uitgeverij SUN, Amsterdam, 2004.

Coastal Quality Studio. *Safety and Quality for the Dutch Coast: Towards 2100*. Atelier Kustkwaliteit, Delft, 2013.

de Monté Verloren, J. P., and J. E. Spruit. *Hoofdlijnen der ontwikkeling der rechterlijke organisatie in de Noordelijke Nederlanden tot de Bataafse omwenteling*. Kluwer, Deventer, 1982.

Denslagen, W. *Romantisch modernisme*. Uitgeverij Sun, Amsterdam, 2004.

Driesprong, A. *Water, gemeenschappen en waterschappen. Wettelijke taken en bevoegdheden in het regional waterbeheer*. SDU Uitgevers, Den Haag, 2004.

Faludi, A., and A. van der Valk. *Rule and Order: Dutch Planning Doctrine in the Twentieth Century*. Kluwer, Dordrecht, 2010.

Hooimeijer, F. L. *The Tradition of Making: Polder Cities*. Doctoral thesis, Delft University of Technology, 2011. www.repository.tudelft.nl.

Kothuis, B., and N. Brand. "Multifunctionele waterkeringen en legitimiteit. De institutionele achtergrond van het streven naar functiecombinatie met waterveiligheid." In *Watergovernance*, edited by B. Kothuis and T. Heems. *De mythe van droge voeten*. Waterworks, Amsterdam, 2012.

Meyer, H. "Composition and Construction of Dutch Delta Cities." In *Delta Urbanism: The Netherlands*, edited by H. Meyer, I. Bobbink, and S. Nijhuis, 64–99. APA Planners Press, Chicago, 2010.

Meyer, V. J., J. van den Berg, A. K. Bregt, R. Broesi, E. Dammers, J. Edelenbos, L. Nieuwenhuijze, G. Roeleveld, and G. Meyer. *Nieuwe perspectieven voor een verstedelijkte delta. Naar een methode van planvorming en ontwerp*. MUST Publishers, Delft, 2013.

Rutte, R. "Groei en krimp van de Hollandse stad." *Overholland* 3 (2006): 29–56.

Steenhuis, M. "De cultuur van de Nederlandse kust: Durf te differentieren" In *Ecologie, cultuur en economie van de Nederlandse kust*, edited by M. Löffler, M. Steenhuis, and M. de Pater, 33–34. Atelier Kustkwaliteit, Delft, 2013.

Stenvert, R., C. Kolman, and S. van Ginkel-Meester, eds. *Monumenten in Nederland. Zuid-Holland*. Waanders Uitgevers, Zwolle, 2004.

Stive, M., and H. Vrijling. "Draining, dredging, reclaiming: The technology of making a dry, safe and sustainable delta landscape." In *Delta Urbanism: The Netherlands*, edited by H. Meyer, I. Bobbink, and S. Nijhuis, 20–43. APA Planners Press, Chicago, 2010.

van Dam, P. J. E. M. "Cities and Flood Control: The Amphibious Culture in the Netherlands before 1800." Introduction and paper presented at the plenary openings panel "Perception and Management of Disastrous Floods" of the

International Water History Association conference, Delft University of Technology, June 17, 2010.

van der Ham, W. "De historie." In *Waterlandschappen, de cultuurhistorie van de toekomst als opgave voor het waterbeheer*, edited by M. van Buuren. Ministerie van V&W-RIZA, Lelystad, 2002.

van der Sande, C. M. *Design of a Dutch Superlevee.* Master's thesis, Delft University of Technology, 2009. www.repository.tudelft.nl.

van Tielhof, M., and P. J. E. M. van Dam. *Waterstaat in stedenland. Het hoogheemraadschap van Rijnland voor 1857.* Matrijs: Utrecht, 2006.

Conclusion

Matthew Pelz

In recent years, a series of severe weather events has instilled a fuller appreciation for the traumatic potential of coastal flooding in historic communities. In these cases, inextricable from the experience of the storm itself is the fear of recurrence and the imagining of even worse storms yet to come. Similar to the way authors Kothuis and Brand identify a long-term evolution in attitudes toward flooding in the Netherlands, we can sense a shift in American perceptions of disasters since the devastation of Hurricane Katrina in 2005. Major storms that followed, including hurricanes Ike, Sandy, and Harvey, brought not only physical devastation, but dread in the awareness that a changing climate renders obsolete our previous beliefs regarding the upper limits of storm force and frequency. As communities across the Gulf and Atlantic coasts confront the challenges of poststorm recovery, they proceed under intense pressure to repair historic buildings and rebuild cities with supreme foresight.

Along with an increased pressure to demonstrate enhanced resilience, the recovery process brings an influx of funding at a scale unimaginable under other circumstances. Our most substantial resilience projects come to fruition in the years immediately following severe disasters when motivation and money are most abundant. Obviously, we would prefer to enact resilience measures *before* the storm and then spend the ensuing years blissfully reaping benefits instead of cleaning up streets and tearing down buildings. But as historical case studies like that of the 1900 Galveston Storm demonstrate, our tendency to be reactive rather than proactive has a long precedent. In the absence of a broader reassessment of planning efforts, the onus is placed on coastal communities to use the opportunities that arise during the years after a disaster to learn from the experience and to adapt more fully to a changing climate.

Unfortunately, urgency in the response and recovery phases is not especially conducive to the development and implementation of innovative, locally driven resilience strategies. In the weeks, months, and years fol-

Heavy rains routinely cause severe flooding in Galveston. This photo, taken after a storm in September 2015, shows flooding along Broadway, the city's main thoroughfare, located ten blocks from the harbor. (Jennifer Reynolds, *Galveston County Daily News*, September 2, 2015)

lowing an event, local leaders are called on to make quick decisions and offer practical guidance to citizens and property owners, with little time for additional research or training. These circumstances manufacture conflict. Environmentally minded experts emphasize a measured, thoroughly studied approach in recognition of long-term, potentially irreversible consequences of mitigation and adaptation strategies. Engineers and builders are more likely to focus on the problem at hand and the multitudes of people whose lives might be improved or even saved through a bold application of ingenuity.

For preservationists, two primary areas of concern have arisen during ongoing recovery projects. First, the environmental costs of large-scale construction efforts are staggering, particularly regarding discarded building materials. Anyone familiar with historic construction practices recognizes the high quality of materials that were used during the nineteenth and early twentieth centuries. In these circumstances, much of that material is certainly damaged or deteriorated, but experience tells us that large portions are repairable. Housing recovery efforts, which typically involve out-of-state planning firms and contractors, include few incentives to maximize material conservation. Instead, deadline-conscious project organizers are pushed toward the simplest alternative—often demolition and reconstruction, with tons of irreplaceable historic materials deposited in landfills. In Galveston, preservation-minded project managers coordinated with the Galveston Historical Foundation to salvage as much historic material as possible from demolished houses. Even with that successful collaboration, it is impossible to estimate the amount of reusable historic materials that were ultimately removed from the island in the years after the storm.

Adding to the environmental costs are the choices we make regarding new construction. Do we opt for energy-efficient construction techniques such as those modeled by Claudette Reichel in Louisiana, or do we instead settle for the quickest and cheapest alternatives? Expressed in those words, a preference for the more sustainable strategy seems obvious, but amid an intense recovery process the choice is not so simple.

The second major worry of preservationists in storm-hit areas concerns cultural heritage in vulnerable neighborhoods. In many coastal communities, historic development patterns place more affluent citizens on higher-elevation land. Working-class families, on the other hand, tend to settle in low-lying areas. Neighborhood residents and architectural historians alike value the houses in these poorer districts for what they tell us about the evolution of American society and for the roles they play in fostering a sense of community. Yet these neighborhoods usually bear the brunt of flood damage, and afterward, their residents face the greatest difficulties in navigating the bureaucracy of housing recovery programs.

The challenges in protecting low-income historic neighborhoods from flooding are not superficial. Through decades of work, preservationists around the country have developed a range of policies and incentives to help communities protect their neighborhoods from unwanted development. In many cases, these policies include provisions against inappropriate architectural treatments, which may include the elevation or relocation of a house. Unfortunately, these are two common flood mitigation strategies. Assuming residents are able to secure assistance for repairs, they may find themselves choosing between preserving the identity of their community and protecting their families from flooding.

The apparent conflict begins to disappear when preservationists work with the understanding that in most cases the intact preservation of historic architectural examples is not the ultimate goal, but rather an important means to a different end—the preservation of cultural heritage. How much does the historic significance of a neighborhood matter if

In Galveston, house moving is a traditional practice for flood mitigation. The Galveston Historical Foundation uses the practice to preserve houses damaged or threatened by flooding. This photo shows two of the five houses that GHF moved between 2016 and 2018. (Michael Guillot, Galveston Historical Foundation, 2016)

proneness to flooding renders its houses uninhabitable? Early preservation leaders developed our existing preservation standards to combat rampant destruction during the second half of the twentieth century, not to protect buildings from storms or to prepare cities for a changing climate. In light of changing circumstances, the reconsideration of these guidelines and the inclusion of more proactive flood adaptation strategies is appropriate and necessary.

The departure from preservation orthodoxy and the embracing of building relocation and aggressive elevation is less disagreeable in Galveston, where mainstay house-moving contractors operated throughout the city's historic periods of development. City officials and property owners worked throughout the nineteenth century to find ways to better protect buildings from flooding and, as examined by Jodi Wright-Gidley, escalated their efforts to an enormous scale after the 1900 Hurricane. Why then would including building relocation as a part of modern efforts constitute a violation of the city's cultural heritage? The Galveston Historical Foundation, having organized the relocation of eight buildings since Hurricane Ike, views these projects as a fulfillment of its mission rather than a lamentable concession to the demands of an emergency. Other coastal communities might have insights of a similar sort in reconsidering their own development histories.

Aside from preservation incentives that might be retuned to encourage enhanced resilience, the field of historic preservation has much to offer in the effort to fortify our coastal cities. The practice of relocating flood-prone buildings, described above, is just one example of a strategy we can borrow from previous generations. We can clearly see the benefits of a retrospective approach in the context of energy-efficient building design. Lacking modern building systems, nineteenth-century builders in hot and humid climates designed houses to maximize natural cooling effects through careful site selection and through the incorporation of features such as high ceilings, large double-sash windows, and vented attics. After abandoning these features during portions of the twentieth century, modern builders have reincorporated them in combination with modern materials and systems to provide comfortable living environments as cleanly and efficiently as possible. A similar dynamic is at play regarding disaster protection and flood mitigation, and modern planners can follow the examples of historic builders who emphasized material quality, design adaptability, and conscientious site selection.

After Hurricane Ike, we were inspired by the work of Claudette Reichel and the LSU AgCenter to explore the climate-conscious aspects of historic buildings. As part of the Green Revival project, we relocated an 1891 house that had been slated for demolition and then rehabilitated it using a combination of preservation practices and green building techniques. We highlighted the aspects of traditional design that make older buildings more resilient and sustainable, and we incorporated new products and systems that could improve their performance. Thousands of visitors toured the house, and many asked for our guidance as they completed repairs on their own houses.

Like others who have lived and worked through severe flooding, we found after Hurricane Ike that with the destruction come opportunities—the potential for innovation and the formation of interdisciplinary collaborations. Our experience during the recovery years spurred us to share our insights and to highlight the projects that have inspired us. This book is the result of a series of conferences we hosted in an effort to form a

In 2010, the Galveston Historical Foundation relocated and rehabilitated this storm-damaged house as a model of sustainability and preservation. The house was certified LEED for Homes Platinum. (Brian M. Davis, Galveston Historical Foundation, 2010)

network of preservationists, engineers, architects, city leaders, and public health experts to educate one another about different aspects of resilience. Through sharing some of their stories, we hope to promote the thoughtful, flexible approach that we have found to be vital in understanding the relationship between our history and our environment. Overlooking this relationship weakens both our ability to preserve our cultural heritage and our capacity to protect our coastal cities.

Contributors

John Anderson is the Maurice Ewing Professor of Oceanography Emeritus at Rice University and the academic director of the Shell Center for Sustainability. His current research interests are in (1) the recent retreat history of the Antarctic Ice Sheet and controls on ice sheet stability as it relates to sea-level rise and (2) the evolution of the US Gulf Coast and response of coastal environments to climate change. John has participated in 24 scientific expeditions to Antarctica and countless other expeditions from Alaska to Chile. He has authored and coauthored over 250 peer-reviewed publications, edited five volumes, and written two books, *Antarctic Marine Geology* (Cambridge University Press) and *Formation and Future of the Upper Texas Coast* (Texas A&M University Press). John is past president of the Society for Sedimentary Research. He has received several awards, including two Rice teaching awards: the Outstanding Educator Award of the Gulf Coast Geological Society and the 2007 Shepard Medal of the Society for Sedimentary Research.

A. D. "Nikki" Brand, PhD, studied human geography at the University of Amsterdam and worked as an urban planner and heritage consultant in the Netherlands. In her PhD work, completed in 2012, she explained the rise of the polycentric Dutch Randstad from the thirteenth century by identifying the instruments and motives of respective governments to influence the competitive positions of cities in their territory.

Dr. Brand combines insights from several disciplines, including spatial planning, domestic administration, economic history, and water management, and is fascinated by the concepts of urban autonomy and path dependency. She is employed as a postdoc with the faculty of Architecture and the Built Environment at the Delft University of Technology, where she investigates how intervention through spatial planning can meet the challenge of territorial management in the context of the growing complexity of networked urban regions. Dr. Brand works in the department of Spatial Planning and Strategy on international case studies and cross-national research on global and European cities and regions, and the planning tools they use.

Additionally, as an independent consultant, Dr. Brand works with Texas A&M University at College Station on a research project evaluating the coordination and responsiveness of community "networks of plans" to coastal flooding hazards in the United States and the Netherlands.

W. Dwayne Jones is a graduate of Trinity University in San Antonio in history and Asian studies. He holds a master's degree in urban and regional planning and historic preservation from George Washington University in Washington, DC. He is executive director of the Galveston Historical Foundation (GHF) (2006–present), one of the nation's largest local preservation nonprofits. The GHF owns or manages 16 historic properties, including several historic vessels, and he also manages museums and community preservation programs. Following Hurricane Ike in 2008, the GHF formed the Center for Coastal Heritage to address preservation issues and techniques unique to historic coastal communities. From 2000 to 2006, he served as executive director of Preservation Dallas, the local nonprofit preservation organization for Dallas. He earned membership in the American Institute of Certified Planners (AICP). Prior to his work with nonprofits, he directed the federal National Register and Certified Local Government programs at the Texas Historical Commission, where he worked for 12 years and held several preservation planning positions at the local level.

B. L. M. "Bee" Kothuis, PhD, is a design anthropologist and holds a PhD in science, technology, and society studies. In her thesis, titled "Flood Safety: Managing Vulnerability beyond the Myth of Dry Feet," she explains Dutch strategies of coping with flood risk.

Dr. Kothuis works as an independent consultant and a researcher at the Delft University of Technology in the Netherlands. She is the research and educational exchange coordinator for Dutch collaboration with Texas-based universities for development of flood risk reduction strategies and the National Science Foundation's Partnerships for International Research and Education (NSF-PIRE). Additionally, she works as a postdoc in two multidisciplinary research programs of the Dutch National Science Foundation: Integral and Sustainable Design of Multifunctional Flood Defenses, and Integral and Sustainable Design of Ports in Africa.

In her academic Action Research projects, Dr. Kothuis develops methods for interdisciplinary knowledge integration within and between academics and public and private stakeholders in research and design projects for flood risk management. Additionally, she develops decision-making support tools for flood risk management, one of which, the Contested Issues Game Structuring Approach (CIGAS), was applied in Texas in 2014. In the Building-with-Nature (BwN) research section at the Delft University of Technology, Dr. Kothuis works on delta, infrastructure, and mobility initiatives, and the development of the BwN Living Lab.

Debbie McNulty is a curious, imaginative, decisive, ambitious architect of strategies to achieve vision. Her professional emphasis is on systems change, equity, and developing the strengths of nonprofit organizations. Her extensive experience includes cultural policy, philanthropy, public-private partnerships, community-based organizations, and the arts. Her career encompasses positions including a consulting practice, director of the Houston Mayor's Office of Cultural Affairs, program officer with the Houston Endowment, and executive director of Art League Houston. She is a senior fellow of the American Leadership Forum Gulf Coast Class XXIII and a founding member of the Harvey Arts Recovery Fund. She volunteers on nonprofit boards and occasionally speaks and writes concerning issues she cares deeply about.

Bruce A. Mowry, PhD, PE, is the former city engineer for Miami Beach, Florida. He has over 35 years of experience working on municipal projects in both the United States and foreign countries. Water resource projects in New Orleans, Santa Barbara/Los Angeles/Southern California, Trinidad and Tobago, Egypt, and mainland China, along with teaching at Louisiana State University in New Orleans (UNO), the University of California, Irvine, and the University of Southern California, are some of the experiences he brings to the city of Miami Beach to assist in improving its infrastructure to meet the climate change and sea-level rise challenges facing it. He holds a PhD in civil engineering from Mississippi State University along with multiple other degrees and certifications.

Hal Needham is the founder and president of Marine Weather and Climate, LLC. He served as the director of the Center for Coastal Heritage and Resiliency at the Galveston Historical Foundation. He led this center in research and outreach related to the intersection of coastal hazards and the built environment. Needham has received three degrees in geography; a BS from Penn State University (1997), an MS from Louisiana State University (2010), and a PhD from Louisiana State University (2014). Most of his work has focused on data-driven storm surge research, starting with the construction of the first comprehensive storm surge database for the US Gulf Coast. Needham currently runs the U-Surge Project, an effort to provide storm surge data and analysis to 50 US cities.

Matthew Pelz has worked for the Galveston Historical Foundation (GHF) since 2009. His primary focus is the integration of resilience and sustainability into historic preservation efforts. During his tenure, the GHF completed the Green Revival House, a historic house rehabilitation that earned platinum certification from LEED for Homes, and developed the Center for Coastal Heritage, which explores the intersection between the natural and built environments in coastal settings. He holds degrees in history from the University of North Carolina at Chapel Hill and in historic preservation from Clemson University and the College of Charleston.

Claudette Hanks Reichel, EdD, is a professor and extension housing specialist with the Louisiana State University AgCenter. She spearheaded and serves as director of the LaHouse Resource Center, a demonstration of high-performance housing solutions, an educational attraction, and a regional hub of Louisiana Extension's sustainable housing educational outreach programs. The vision of LaHouse is to "shape our future" with resource-efficient, durable, healthy, convenient, and practical homes for the southern climate and natural hazards.

Since 1981, Dr. Reichel has developed numerous educational outreach materials, programs, and delivery systems relating to housing and building science, including energy efficiency, indoor air quality, hurricane and flood resilience, home-buyer education, and others. She has authored more than 100 extension publications, including *Building Your High Performance Home—Gulf Region Homeowners Guide*. Dr. Reichel has received 12 national and state awards for program excellence, was twice a featured speaker at the National Building Museum in Washington, DC, and has presented at numerous national and regional events.

Jodi Wright-Gidley earned a bachelor's degree from Baylor University and a master's from Sam Houston State University. She became director of the Galveston County Historical Museum just in time to witness the destruction left behind by Hurricane Ike in 2008. Storm surge inundated the building, resulting in closure of the museum. During the precarious year of recovery from Hurricane Ike, Wright-Gidley and Jennifer Marines coauthored *Galveston: A City on Stilts*, which features a large collection of photographs taken during the city's seawall construction and grade raising in the early 1900s.

Index

Other Books in the Gulf Coast Books Series

Lighthouses of Texas
Lindsay T. Baker and F. R. Holland

Laguna Madre of Texas and Tamaulipas
John W. Tunnell and Frank W. Judd

Fishing Yesterday's Gulf Coast
Barney Farley and Larry McEachron

Designing the Bayous: The Control of Water in the Atchafalaya Basin, 1800–1995
Martin Reuss

Life on Matagorda Island
Wayne H. McAlister and Martha K. McAlister

Book of Texas Bays
Jim Blackburn and Jim Olive

Plants of the Texas Coastal Bend
Roy L. Lehman and Tammy White

Galveston Bay
Sally E. Antrobus

Crossing the Rio Grande: An Immigrant's Life in the 1880s
Luis G. Gómez and Guadalupe Valdez

Birdlife of Houston, Galveston, and the Upper Texas Coast
Ted Eubanks and Robert A. Behrstock

Formation and Future of the Upper Texas Coast: A Geologist Answers Questions about Sand, Storms, and Living by the Sea
John B. Anderson

Finding Birds on the Great Texas Coastal Birding Trail: Houston, Galveston, and the Upper Texas Coast
Ted Eubanks and Robert A. Behrstock

Texas Coral Reefs
Jesse Cancelmo and Sylvia Earle

Fishes of the Texas Laguna Madre: A Guide for Anglers and Naturalists
David A. McKee and Henry Compton

Louisiana Coast: Guide to an American Wetland
Gay M. Gomez

Storm over the Bay: The People of Corpus Christi and Their Port
Mary J. O'Rear

After Ike: Aerial Views from the No-Fly Zone
Bryan Carlile

Kayaking the Texas Coast
John Whorff

Glory of the Silver King: The Golden Age of Tarpon Fishing
Hart Stilwell

River Music: An Atchafalaya Story
Ann McCutchan

Del Pueblo: A History of Houston's Hispanic Community
Thomas H. Kreneck

Letters to Alice: Birth of the Kleberg-King Ranch Dynasty
Jane Clements Monday and Francis Brannen Vick

Hundred Years of Texas Waterfowl Hunting: The Decoys, Guides, Clubs, and Places, 1870s to 1970s
R. K. Sawyer

Texas Market Hunting: Stories of Waterfowl, Game Laws, and Outlaws
R. K. Sawyer

Fire in the Sea: Bioluminescence and Henry Compton's Art of the Deep
David A. McKee

Pioneering Archaeology in the Texas Coastal Bend: The Pape-Tunnell Collection
John W. Tunnell and Jace Tunnell

Vertical Reefs: Life on Oil and Gas Platforms in the Gulf of Mexico
Mary Katherine Wicksten

Glorious Gulf of Mexico: Life Below the Blue
Jesse Cancelmo

Alligators of Texas
Louise Hayes and Philippe Henry

Bulwark Against the Bay: The People of Corpus Christi and Their Seawall
Mary Jo O'Rear

Texan Plan for the Texas Coast
James B. Blackburn

Dr. Arthur Spohn: Surgeon, Inventor, and Texas Medical Pioneer
Jane Clements Monday

Fishes of the Rainbow: Henry Compton's Art of the Reefs
David A. McKee